From Reporter to Refugee

The Law of Asylum in Great Britain
A Personal Account

WorldView Publishing in association with
the Refugee Studies Programme, Oxford University

Copyright © Victor Lal, 1997

All rights reserved.

No part of this book may be reproduced in any form or by any means, electronic or mechanical, including photocopying, recording, or information storage and retrieval system, without prior permission in writing from the publisher.

A British Library Cataloguing in Publication record is available for this book

ISBN 1 872142 28 1   hardback
ISBN 1 872142 29 X   paperback

Published by WorldView Publishing,
P.O. Box 595, Oxford OX2 6YH, UK

Design and typesetting by Tom Dyson,
WorldView Publications

Printed and bound in the United Kingdom

Dedication
To my wife Beathe and daughter Bianca who are cheerfully sharing my burden of exile in Norway, and to my family 'marooned at home' in Fiji Islands which is my birthplace and true home.

And to all those who share my fight for freedom, justice, and human rights.

Contents

Introduction
Alasdair Mackenzie, Asylum Aid, London   v

Part One
From Fiji to Oxford: A Journey Shattered   1

Part Two
The Law of Asylum in England   9

Part Three
From Reporter to Refugee: 'A Babylonian World'   49

"An opponent of a dictator is an enemy of the state"

W. Ivor Jennings, *The Law and the Constitution*

Refugees and the Nobel Peace Prize

The Norwegian Nobel Committee has awarded the Peace Prize for 1981 to the Office of the United Nations High Commissioner for Refugees. The award of the Prize this year is one of the very few occasions on which one and the same organisation will be receiving the Nobel Peace Prize for the second time. The first time this occurred was in 1955.

Never have so many millions of people been driven from their native lands as the case is today. We may well entertain a vision of a world without refugees – a world in which men and women are never in jeopardy on account of their religion, their nationality, their political views, or their membership of any group, of a world in which people need never flee from war and civil strife. But this is not the sort of world in which we live. We can so easily be seized by despair or cynicism, by the wish to cultivate our own garden and to be sufficient unto ourselves.

In the years that lie ahead, too, we shall encounter men and women on the run. It is beyond the capacity of mankind to predict where and when new refugee problems will arise. But we possess the fundamental ideas on human rights and a sense of fellow feeling that goes beyond countries and continents, religions, cultures, and racial borders.

We have a duty to the refugees, and this duty is a duty to ourselves and the very basis of our own existence.

The Norwegian Nobel Committee, 1981

Introduction

United Kingdom practices in dealing with refugees and asylum seekers have become increasingly restrictive in recent years. In its zeal to exclude as many asylum seekers as possible, the British Government has resorted to unfair methods to refuse asylum, even to those who obviously merit it.

The case of Victor Lal provides an excellent example. Although the British authorities, perhaps mindful of the potential outcry, never directly attempted to force him, as a renowned dissident, to go back to Fiji, they placed obstacles in his way which a lesser person might not have had the nerve, the stamina, or the widespread support from others on which Victor Lal was able to rely. Having made him wait for years for an initial decision, the Home Office Asylum Division bizarrely denied him refugee status on the grounds that 'information' obtained by the British authorities indicated that he would not be persecuted in Fiji. Instead, he was given the secondary status of exceptional leave to remain, with a right of appeal which Victor Lal unsurprisingly exercised.

What this 'information' was, and by whom and from whom it was obtained, was never made clear. The Home Office, to put it gently, is not above ignoring or even misrepresenting the evidence before it, nor is it always fussy about whose evidence it relies upon. In one recent case, information from a senior official in the Sudanese secret police was proffered by the Home Office as 'evidence' of the true human rights situation in Sudan; whether Sitiveni Rabuka, the coup leader and later Prime Minister of Fiji, was consulted as to his intentions vis-a-vis the person of Victor Lal remains an intriguing question.

If the Home Office's decision on Victor Lal represented a clear breach of natural justice, the determination of the independent adjudicator (now retired) who heard Victor Lal's initial appeal was scarcely better. His approach exemplified the often high-handed approach of adjudicators to the refugees appearing before them. Apart from effectively suggesting that a person who stuck his neck out to criticise a repressive government deserved what he got, he accused Victor Lal, despite his impeccable credentials, of exaggerating his fear of persecution. He was patronising in his dismissal of the experts who had written in Victor Lal's support.

As so often, it was only the Immigration Appeals Tribunal, in considering Victor Lal's appeal against the adjudicator's decision which took a sensible view of the case and directed that it be reheard – although the Tribunal members had clearly been riled by the adjudicator's remarkable decision to add his unsolicited comments on the form appealing against his own determination. Yet it is the Tribunal whose powers are to be curtailed by the legislation brought forward by the British government in 1996.

Victor Lal got justice in the end, when the Home Office caved in under the weight of the evidence in his favour. But in 1996, the probability is that an increasingly shameless government would have few qualms about trying to deport Victor Lal – as witness its performance in the case of a Saudi dissident, Mohamed Al-Masari. Safeguards against injustice for refugees are being stripped away, and the supposedly neutral decision-making process has become a conveyor belt of often outrageous negative decisions. For those less well informed and less articulate than Victor Lal, the position is dire.

Alisdair Mackenzie
Director, Asylum Aid

From Fiji to Oxford

A Journey Shattered

On 14 May 1987, the Indo-Fijians awoke to mark the 108th anniversary of the arrival, aboard the sailing ship *Leonidas*, of the first Indian 'coolies' (labourers) in Fijian waters – among them was my great-great-grandfather – brought by the British from colonial India in 1879 to toil on the sugar plantations as 'overseas bonded labourer in exile'. The month of May 1987 had an additional significance because, for the first time, the descendants of Indo-Fijian labourers were sharing political power with a group of progressive and liberal indigenous Fijians. The previous month, on 12 April, one of the longest reigning democratic governments in the Commonwealth, that of Prime Minister Ratu Sir Kamisese Mara's Alliance Party, had finally conceded defeat to a coalition of parties led by a 52-year-old medical doctor and an indigenous Fijian, Dr Timoci Bavadra, in Fiji's fifth post-independence general election.

The country was being governed by the Indo-Fijian dominated National Federation Party and the multi-racial Fiji Labour Party coalition government. The outcome of the election seemed to promise a new era of multi-racial politics in Fiji. For many traditional Fijian chiefs the results signified the beginning of 'Indo-Fijian rule' but for many Indo-Fijians a dream had finally come true, a share in the political kingdom. That month, however, was to see the arrest of all this progress. A group of ten masked and armed soldiers – led by the country's third-ranking Fijian soldier – Sitiveni Rabuka – stormed Parliament and later declared military rule throughout Fiji. Indo-Fijians were never again to rule Fiji. In short, the Fijian coup d'etat of May 1987, in a cruel twist of fate, arrested the Indo-Fijian

2 *From Reporter to Refugee*

community's triumphant march from plantation to Fiji's parliament.

The racist coup also shattered my planned return journey from Oxford to Fiji, and forced me to travel down an unfamiliar road into exile. But, unlike my great-great-grandparents, I was filled with a belief that Fiji was (and still is) as much mine by 'right of vision' as it is mine by 'right of birth'. This conviction has been kept aglow by the testament of my 'coolie' forebears as narrated in the poems (*Voices in the River*, 1985) of the Indo-Fijian academic and the politician, Satendra Nandan, who was among those to be seized in Parliament on 14 May 1987:

> in the shadow of a tamarind tree
> in the cawcaw of a crow
> like a scarecrow
> lay an old, old man –
>
> dead, asleep, or just dreaming...
> from his eyes I saw a ghost arise
> and walk beside me
> as a scar on the soul.
>
> the voice deafened my ears:
> young man, you see me skin and bones
> like a sugar sack full of stones
> but once...
> youth I lost here, and grace
> I gave to this island place
> what more than a man's age
> can one give to history's outrage?
> with the faith I lived,
> I fashioned a new world
> with bits from the old.
>
> the Himalayas where the pandavas perished
> in my old song I have carried;
> centuries flow in my blood
> civilisations born before the flood;

I have lived this exile
more gloriously than Rama
and built kingdoms, you may find,
nobler than Ajodhya
in my ancient, eternal mind!

pity not me then
nor mourn for a dying, decrepit man:
think of what I was
and what you can be
for I only hope
as I see you grope
your journey from here
will be without fear
as mine might have been.

The following pages recount my seven-year battle with the British government to obtain political asylum, the destructive force this process has on human dignity and human rights, and the ultimate journey into exile. There was a serious temptation to regard the whole asylum saga as an unpleasant episode best forgotten; but there were (and still are) hundreds, perhaps thousands, like me in a similar predicament. This book is the outcome, after long hesitation on my part, of the urging of a number of sympathisers, to proclaim with urgency the truth about the ordeal (and the peril) of applying for political asylum in the United Kingdom.

To understand the foregoing chronology of events, it is necessary to consider briefly my own arrival, reception, and initial rejection for political asylum in Great Britain. In September 1984, the Air New Zealand jumbo jet on which I was travelling landed at Gatwick Airport. Shortly afterwards, I stepped out of the business-class seat (courtesy of Reuters News Agency) into a cold and wintery England, leaving behind the warmth of my native Fiji. The cold of England was, however, warmed with English hospitality. The reception was courteous; the immigration officer at Gatwick treated me with civility. He had never seen a Fijian passport but had a fairly impressive image of the many Fijian islands floating like a handful of confetti in the South Pacific.

Outside, in the arrival lounge at Gatwick, the chauffeur from Reuters was waiting for me with a big placard with my name inscribed on it. As I got into the car for Oxford University, it finally dawned on me that I was now in England, a country which had not only existed in my history and geography school books but had dominated every aspect of my life in Fiji. I had seen Princess Anne and Prince Charles in Fiji in the 1970s, and had an audience with their mother, Her Majesty the Queen in the 1980s. Now, I felt as if the Empire's stepchild had come 'home', even though I had only arrived to study on a Reuters fellowship at Oxford.

In any case, my passport was meant to afford me protection. It stated:

> 'The Governor-General and Commander-in-Chief in and over Fiji requests and requires in the Name of Her Majesty the Queen all those whom it may concern to allow the bearer to pass freely without let or hindrance and to afford the bearer such assistance and protection as may be necessary.'

Although Fiji had shrugged off British colonial rule in 1970, the monarchical magic still bewitched the citizens of Fiji. The Queen remained the constitutional head of Fiji (until the 1987 coups); the British flag merged with the newly independent flag of Fiji, and Her Majesty continued to stare in our faces from the coins and notes in circulation in post-independent Fiji. Moreover, every year the nation – in the form of public holidays – celebrated Her Majesty's as well as her son Prince Charles's birthdays. In other words, although the Fijian chiefs had secured independence, they declined to sever dependence on the British monarchy. Fiji's national Coat of Arms consists the motto 'Rerevaka na Kalou ka Doka na Tui': 'Fear God and honour the Queen'.

Ironically, I was following in the footsteps of three great Fijian chiefs and political leaders of pre- and post-independence Fiji who, during their colonial careers, had studied at Oxford: the late Ratu Sir Lala Sukuna, the first Speaker of the Fiji Legislative Council; Ratu Sir Kamisese Mara, the Prime Minister (now President) of Fiji; and Ratu Sir Penaia Ganilau, the Governor-General, and later President of post-coup Fiji. In particular, Mara and Ganilau would later change and reshape my identity in Fiji.

The academic world of Oxford was a great change (and temporary refuge) from the hurly-burly of my life working as a senior sub-editor-cum-investigative-journalist on the *Fiji Sun* newspaper and general secretary of the Journalists' Association in Fiji. The independent *Fiji Sun* was the first newspaper to be shut down by the military, and later ceased operations in Fiji altogether after its owners in Hong Kong and New Zealand refused to operate under military censorship. Many of my colleagues were harassed, assaulted, and even detained, during the coup. Many of the overseas staff were deported and some of the local journalists were forced into exile. The *Fiji Sun*'s deputy publisher was arrested and thrown in the same prison as Bavadra, the deposed Prime Minister, and members of his Cabinet. A New Zealander, he was later ordered to leave Fiji. The other newspaper, *The Fiji Times*, owned by the press baron Rupert Murdoch, agreed to operate under partial 'military oversight'.

At Oxford, I encountered two types of academic: those who held a romantic view of my islands, and those who had had some dealings with the country and her political leaders. Among the latter was an Oxford academic, who invited me for lunch at one of the colleges. He had dealt with the Fijian political leaders in the 1960s and was a special guest of one of them in Fiji. By the time we had finished the lunch, it was decided, on the basis of what I had told him, that I should write a study of race and ethnic politics in Fiji.

On 3 June 1986, at a seminar on Ethnic, Cultural and Racial Studies at St Antony's College, organised by Professor Kenneth Kirkwood, the then Rhodes Professor of Race Relations, and who had a fairly good grasp of pre-independence Fijian politics, I made the first and most prophetic prediction of the state of things to happen in the coming months: 'The Politics of Communalism in Fiji: The Coming Coup.'

As already stated, on 14 May 1987, Sitiveni Rabuka (now Prime Minister of Fiji) stood up in the Parliament of Fiji to declare to the politicians, the nation and the world:

> Sit down everybody, sit down. This is a take-over. We apologise for any inconvenience caused. You are requested to stay cool, stay down, sit down and listen to what we are going to tell you. Please stay calm, ladies and gentlemen ...

He claimed that it was the calling of God to execute the coup, and to rewrite the Constitution of Fiji in order to prevent the majority Indo-Fijian population from ever capturing political power again. They were to be legally discriminated against in every walk of life and hence were to be subservient to the indigenous Fijians, especially to the traditional Fijian chiefs. In other words, democracy died in Fiji on 14 May 1987 and with it, my hopes of returning home.

It was also the beginning of a long and seemingly endless struggle to secure refuge in my 'imagined home' in England, and to join a long list of political dissidents in exile. In the meantime, between May and September 1987, the military, supported by the Fijian chiefs (Ratu Mara and Ratu Penaia Ganilau) imposed a racist Constitution which curtailed the political and human rights of my people – the Indo-Fijians – in Fiji. The President, Ratu Ganilau, echoing the high-priest and architect of racism in South Africa, Dr H.F. Verwoerd, affirmed the primacy of race in post-coup Fiji, when he declared:

> We want the Indians and Europeans to continue to run their business but we [native Fijians] must have political dominance at all times ... We will not sacrifice political

leadership of [our] country nor at the same time accept the [paramount position] of other races.

He was supported by Ratu Mara who insisted that the 1990 Constitution addressed 'the rights and aspirations' of the Fijian population.

These pronouncements, however, did not represent the majority opinion. As a Maori professor, Ranginui Walker, declared in Auckland, New Zealand, in 1987,

> The coup is nothing more than a shameful use by an oligarchy that refuses to recognise and accept the winds of change in Fiji. It would appear from this distance that the Great Council of Chiefs, still living in their traditional ways, have been misled. Their land rights are secure under the [1970] constitution. But because they have not been taught their rights they are readily manipulated and swayed by demagogues.

His condemnations were disregarded as the racist Fijian chiefs, intellectuals and the military introduced their own version of apartheid in a South Pacific paradise.

But who would provide refuge to me? The most obvious and immediate host was Her Majesty's Government in Great Britain. From my childhood, and later at school and other state occasions, I was taught to sing 'God Save Our Gracious Queen'. Now I was singing to Her Majesty's British Government, 'Save Me From the Dictators in Fiji'. Were they going to respond to my call? Was there protection under the Union Jack (also fluttering in the left-hand corner of the Fiji flag) from the winds of Fijian racism? Was I going to be reluctantly transformed from Reporter to Refugee?

The Law of Asylum in Great Britain

The thought of applying for political asylum in Great Britain was extremely unpalatable and frightening, for many of my sympathisers feared that I could end up being locked away along with up to 100 Sri Lankan Tamils then held on board a disused Channel car ferry, the *Earl William*. Others felt that I might be detained at the pleasure of Her Majesty in one of the many prisons around England, a common feature of government policy as a deterrent to potential asylum seekers. Some even feared that I might die in custody. In the end, and after months of agonising over the state of affairs in Fiji, I was advised by Rights and Justice in London (now Asylum Aid) to file an application for political asylum in England on the grounds of a well-founded fear of persecution in Fiji by reason of race, religion, nationality, membership of a particular social or political opinion, under the terms of the 1951 United Nations Convention relating to the Status of Refugees, the main instrument governing refugee protection. In December 1987, Mary Dines, then director of Rights and Justice, who had previously helped the Ugandan Asian refugees, filed an application for politician asylum on my behalf.

During the next years, I wrote various personal articles, made broadcasts, and gave seminars and talks, all condemning the May and September 1987 coups and the racist political developments in post-coup Fiji. In 1990, my study of Fijian politics was published as *Fiji: Coups in Paradise – Race, Politics and Military Intervention* (Zed Books, London, and Allied Publishers, New Delhi).

The ordeal of waiting for a decision for asylum is a long, arduous, and painfully frustrating experience. Indeed, the

British Home Office took three long years to relay its initial decision. On 8 August 1990, it notified me that the application for refugee status had been carefully considered but refused. No reasons were furnished. However, I was granted exceptional leave to remain (ELR) in the United Kingdom until 8 August 1991 outside the Immigration Rules instead of under Paragraph 139 of HC169 because of 'the particular circumstances of the case'. It did not mention, however, that the first year of exceptional leave, a status which has to be renewed every year, was to run out on 8th August 1991 because of the 'disappearance' of my passport, sent by recorded delivery to the Home Office. The notice was reserved on 13 December 1990 as there was doubt about the validity of the first service.

On 13 December 1990, the Home Office again notified me of the variation of leave to remain in the United Kingdom until 8 August 1991. I was also informed of the right to appeal under Section 14(1) of the Immigration Act 1971 to the appellate authorities within 14 days against the refusal of refugee status. The advantages of full refugee status, as opposed to exceptional leave, are not very great, but I wished to appeal nonetheless. Those with refugee status get indefinite leave to remain (settlement) after four years; those with ELR have to wait for seven years. A week later, on 21 December, I lodged the Notice of Appeal to an adjudicator and delegated Alasdair Mackenzie of Asylum Aid as my official representative. On application, I was granted further exceptional leave to remain in the United Kingdom, this time with expiry date of 8 August 1992.

With exceptional leave to remain, certain conditions were placed and benefits granted. First, I was specifically informed that I should fully understand that if during my stay in the United Kingdom, I took part in activities involving, for example, the support or encouragement of violence, or conspiracy to cause violence, whether in the United Kingdom or abroad, the Secretary of State 'may curtail your stay or deport you'. The grant of exceptional leave to remain did not entitle my spouse or children under 18 to join me. An application for them to do so could not normally be considered until four years from the date of this letter. This was subject to my having received further grants of exceptional leave. The normal requirements of the Immigration Rules regarding support and accommodation of relatives would have to be satisfied. An application for family reunion 'may be granted at an earlier point if there are compelling compassionate circumstances'.

What constitutes 'compelling circumstances' is a very vague and discretionary concept, as shown vividly in the case of a Bosnian Muslim refugee, Hamdija Subonjic, who came to Great Britain after being rescued from a detention camp. The Home Office told him that his wife, Safija, could join him but that his two daughters – Azra and Mirzeta – could not. Safija refused to leave Bosnia without her daughters and in May 1993, she and Mirzeta were captured by Serbs, raped and murdered.[1] Fortunately, I was still a bachelor at that time so the 'family reunion' clause did not affect me, even though my widowed mother and other members of the family were living a very precarious existence in Fiji.

Furthermore, I was notified that if I travelled abroad, the leave that I was now being granted would lapse. Any application to return 'will be considered as an application for fresh leave'. The end result of this condition was that I remained stranded in the United Kingdom from 1987 to 1993. I was also advised to keep my Fiji passport valid. If, however, my national authorities would not renew or replace my passport, or I could show that it would be unreasonable to expect me to approach my Embassy or Consulate in London, I could apply for a Home Office travel document. We will return to this aspect of the condition later on.

I was, however, notified that I did not need the permission of the Department of Employment or the Home Office before taking a job. I was also free to set up business. Moreover, I was free to use the National Health Service, the social services and other help provided by local authorities as I needed them. All I had to do was to 'take this letter with you and show it if there is any question about your entitlement to the services'.

The terms and conditions of generosity/hospitality, and the availability of entitlements, seemed very attractive and reasonable, at least on paper. The reality was quite different. For example, I found out that many prospective employers and foundations providing research grants, declined to support me on the grounds that I had a very tenuous and unpredictable right to stay in the United Kingdom. The only jobs that seemed to be available to me were of a menial and highly exploitative nature. In other words, I could become effectively a 'coolie' like my indentured forebears, and earn a pittance. Also, some academics and institutions now began to view me as a possible, and perhaps perpetual, burden and therefore tried to distance themselves from me.

A few politely declined to support my application for jobs and research grants, and one director of a reputable research centre at Oxford, a very close acquaintance of mine, even attempted to pre-empt my application for a research grant. A few members of his staff also began to form their own stereotypical images of me, as one of them, Ms A (name withheld), in a characteristic but intriguing conversation, told me years later, in 1996, as follows:

> It's nice to see you after nearly two years. We were so tired of your face. I used to say to Ms B (name withheld), 'Here comes the permanent furniture of the department'.

Sad and bitter, I struggled to laugh off her uncontrolled and shameful admission. As a matter of fact, the majority of the staff at the department had never bothered to support me or remotely shared in my personal dilemmas. Anyway, I had made a personal point of revealing a confident face, to preserve my faith and dignity. For after all, the human face expresses the gamut of our emotions: confidence, anxiety, fear, resentment, pain, happiness, desire, affection and even duplicity, as shamelessly expressed over the years on the face of Ms A towards me.

Meanwhile, I politely reminded Ms A and a few others within our ear-shot the remarks of a Russian dissident who had survived the Gulag prison camps,

> I think that many people in the Western countries have forgotten what freedom and democracy really are. To them, they have become part of a comfortable and undemanding way of life, to achieve a high standard of living, to have a good time. But I am afraid that many forget that democracy and freedom are above all the right to fight. Remember that your freedom ends at that point where your solidarity with the persecuted ends.[2]

In another instance, the then director of the Journalists' Fellowship Programme at Oxford even rebuked me in a letter for recalling my past links with the international news organisation Reuters in an interview with *The Times* newspaper of London in 1988. Perhaps he did not want to jeopardise Reuters' presence in post-coup Fiji; even though its 'man on the spot', a local indigenous Fijian journalist, was a mouthpiece of the military who later co-authored the coup leader's book *Rabuka: No Other Way* (1988). I felt that the world was beginning to turn its back on me. These minor episodes dramatically demonstrated to me the familiar pangs of the 'Song of Exile', 'Exile is the ego that shrinks for how can you prove what you were and what you did? Exile is the erasure of pride.'

There was also no possibility of me starting a business. In fact, the 'unexpected' coup had left me penniless and nearly homeless. In May 1987, I had already begun packing my possessions to return to Fiji, and had, therefore, exhausted my finances. In any case, I had a highly lucrative and respectable job awaiting me in Fiji, so the question of money never crossed my mind. I was planning to leave England on 28 May, but the coup altered my plans, and my life.

As regards financial help from the Benefits Office, I was informed that I was not eligible for monetary support unless my asylum status was confirmed by the Home Office. This it failed to do, despite three requests for verification of my immigration status from the Benefits Office to the Home Office, dating from November 1987, in respect of a claim for benefit from me. For some years, I had to rely on close friends, colleagues, the Quakers, charities for the homeless (and even the much-ridiculed Hare Krishna devotees' vegetarian food) for day to day survival.

The housing officials at the Oxford City Council also displayed contempt and hostility, and one woman officer even disparagingly questioned me as follows: 'Where did you get the money to buy such expensive clothes?'. (I was wearing a Reuters tie, and a second-hand jumper and a blazer from Oxfam charity shop). In reply, I asked her whether she would have treated me differently if I had walked into the office naked! I told her that although I had been stripped of my rights in Fiji, I was not devoid of self-respect and dignity, and that she should treat people with respect. In response, she claimed that the vast majority of refugees or to-be-refugees were cheats, a chilling remark later echoed by a Tory minister, himself the son of a law professor turned refugee from Franco's Spain. I soon concluded that I had a long uphill struggle for basic human survival in the United Kingdom..

The year 1991 was for me a year of anxiety and distress. It was also the year when the British government published its long-awaited Asylum Bill promising a thorough review of asylum policy and its practice in the United Kingdom. On 2 July 1991 the Home Secretary of the time, Kenneth Baker, had announced the controversial new proposals for the treatment of asylum seekers in the United Kingdom. *The Daily Mail* and other newspapers had already paved the way with scurrilous articles on 'bogus refugees'. From a purely professional journalistic point of view, I found these articles crude and nauseating, and feel that they revealed the ugly side of gutter British journalism at its 'best' to the world.

The revulsion was compensated, however, when I learnt in March 1992 that the Amnesty International Journalists' Network, launched officially in London on 21 March, had already adopted the cases of more than 20 journalists throughout the world who had been tortured, threatened or killed because of their work. The Network was set up to enable journalists in the United Kingdom to campaign on behalf of journalists overseas who suffer human rights abuses.

Moreover, Amnesty International assured me of its full support concerning my application for political asylum in Great Britain. A personal meeting with two of Africa's best known dissident writers – the poet Jack Mapanje, whose poems had landed him in a Malawi jail without charge or trial for almost four years, and the Kenyan writer Ngugi Wa Thiongo, who spent one year without trial in a prison in Kenya – strengthened my deeply held conviction and crusade against racism and dictatorship in Fiji.

The 1991 Asylum Bill, intended to ensure 'a substantial acceleration and simplification of the procedures used to deal with applications for asylum', had contained the following proposals:

- the removal of legal aid eligibility in asylum cases;
- the imposition of time limits (48 hours) on the submission of information in support of asylum claims;
- the extension of appeal rights to all asylum seekers, but with the creation of a 'fast-track' procedure to deal with applications which the Home Office considers to be 'clearly unfounded', with no oral hearing on appeal;
- the doubling of fines imposed on airlines bringing in asylum seekers lacking valid documentation, including a valid visa for the UK;
- the establishment of additional document checks at points of embarkation abroad, including sending 'document specialists' to advise airline staff on the validity of passengers' documents.

The British government's rationale for introducing such radical legislation was to curb the enormous rise in asylum applications in the United Kingdom which had taken place over the previous few years. The number of people seeking asylum in the United Kingdom had undoubtedly risen significantly in recent years – from 5,000 in 1988 to 25,000 in 1990 – and Kenneth Baker had cited this increase as the justification for his proposals. He had also argued that 'a growing proportion' of asylum seekers were not 'genuine refugees'. The Bill however met widespread criticism from the House of Lords, the United Nations High Commissioner for Refugees and many other organisations. It also failed to reach the statute books owing to the dissolution of Parliament on 16 March (unfinished legislation cannot be carried over to new Parliament) on the calling of the general election in April 1992.[3]

On 5 September 1991, the year in which the number of applications for political asylum in the United Kingdom was higher than ever before, and fewer applications were received in Britain than in any European country, Asylum Aid had sent a copy of *Fiji: Coups in Paradise* to the Home Office. A month later, on 23 October, it sent a dossier of papers containing evidence covering several years, including letters in support of my asylum claim from leading academics, and from a former coup plotter and Fijian Cabinet minister; a run-down of my academic and journalistic activities, which would put me at risk of being singled out for persecution by the Fijian government; reviews of my book; news reports about the coup and its aftermath, including the kidnap and torture of an Indian academic, Dr Anirudh Singh; Amnesty International reports on human rights abuses by the Fijian authorities; and copies of articles written by me for the *Fiji Sun* newspaper.

Furthermore, Alasdair Mackenzie tried to impress upon the Home Office officials that,

> . . . as the author of a book highly critical of the Fijian regime, as a former journalist with the *Fiji Sun*, and as an ethnic Indian, Victor Lal would be a prime target for persecution. The article from *Melanesia in Review*, which I [Mackenzie] am also appending, shows that the Fijian government is continuing to become more authoritarian and more racist in its attitudes towards the ethnic Indian

population of Fiji (Indo-Fijians). You will note that Mr Lal's paper, the *Fiji Sun*, has now closed down and many of the country's journalists have been persecuted.

We also reminded the Home Office about the new Internal Security Decree which empowered Rabuka, as Minister for Internal Security, to 'order the detention of any persons for up to two years; order restriction of movement, freedom of expression, employment, residence or activity; and prohibit the printing, publication, sale, issue, circulation or possession of any written material, and prohibit its communication through word of mouth'. This extraordinary range of powers violated international standards of human rights. In the light of all this evidence confirming my fears of persecution, Asylum Aid hoped that the Secretary of State would see fit to grant me refugee status.

On 7 November, Asylum Aid submitted further evidence including a list of my publications and broadcasts, a photograph of me at a demonstration in London outside the Fiji embassy against the racist coup, confirmation of various seminars and speeches including one at the British Foreign and Commonwealth Office in London and various press cuttings about Fiji, all relating to persecution in Fiji dated after 26 October 1987, especially the New York-based Committee to Protect Journalists' (CPJ) report which had singled out Fiji for 'special concern'. In its world-wide survey, the CPJ had cited 20 examples of attacks on the Fiji press. The materials were sent to the Home Office with a supplementary note urging them to reconsider their decision in the light of new evidence before a date was set for an appeal hearing.

The Home Office officials refused to change their mind about the refusal and the appeal was set to go ahead. On 6 April 1992 the Home Office issued an explanatory statement notifying me that:

> On 30 April 1990 information was obtained by the Home Office to the effect that conditions had improved in Fiji since the appellant's papers had been prepared, and that the appellant, if he went back to Fiji, would be unlikely to

face anything worse than a reluctance by the authorities to give him a fair chance in any competition for government-related employment. (Britain is a signatory to the Universal Declaration of Human Rights, the UN Convention on Civil and Political Rights, UN Convention Against Torture and the Fourth Protocol to the European Convention on Human Rights).

The Secretary of State then considered the application in the light of all the information before him. Recent information was to the effect that the appellant would, if he went back to Fiji, be unlikely to encounter anything worse than discrimination in employment.

On all the evidence, the Secretary of State could not be satisfied that the appellant's fear of persecution in Fiji was well-founded and he, therefore, refused the application.

Commenting on the 7th November 1991 enclosures, the Home Office disclosed that it had 'obtained further information to the effect that there were no grounds for suspecting the appellant would suffer persecution because of his writing and broadcasting'. As a result, 'the Secretary of State considered the grounds of appeal and the more recent correspondence but could find no reason to alter his decision'. The Appeal was to proceed.

A close examination of the Home Office judgement reveals that, while it denied me the right to asylum, it nevertheless appeared to accept that I would suffer discrimination in employment in Fiji. It, however, refused to explain why I would be discriminated against. In fact, we later expanded on this issue, suggesting to the Home Office that even this would amount to persecution under the 1951 UN Convention. In the Handbook to the Convention, persecution is stated in paragraph 54 to include 'serious restrictions on (an asylum applicant's) right to earn a livelihood', while paragraph 55 goes on to say that,

> Where measures of discrimination are in themselves not of a serious character, they may nevertheless give rise to a reasonable fear of persecution if they produce, in the

mind of the person concerned, a feeling of apprehension and insecurity as regards his future existence.

Alasdair Mackenzie argued:

> I must suggest that the events in Fiji cannot fail to give Mr Lal the feeling of apprehension, giving rise to a well-founded fear of persecution, described in the Handbook. Even if the problems awaiting him did not amount to any more than discrimination, which he does not accept, such discrimination, seen cumulatively, would be of such a serious and far-reaching nature as to amount to persecution under the Convention.

In the light of these representations, and of the information which I had enclosed, the Home Office was requested to review the decision to refuse my application against asylum before the case came up before the Adjudicator again.

Moreover, while the Home Office had written that they refused my application on the basis of 'information' received, they did not specify what information they received, or from whom, and they had provided no examples of it. I felt that it was quite outrageous that they should be able to get away with refusing my application on the basis of secret 'information' which we might be able to challenge if we saw it. Therefore, Mackenzie and I felt that we should request an oral hearing of my appeal, so that we could argue my case in front of an adjudicator, and so that the adjudicator could get an idea of me.

One Oxford academic supporter of mine, after reading the Home Office judgement, even wrote to the Home Secretary at the time, Kenneth Clarke:

> An explanatory statement setting out the reasons for the refusal has now been sent out by the Asylum Division. It notes, among other things, that 'information was obtained by the Home Office' to the effect that Mr Lal would be unlikely to be persecuted in Fiji. No indication has been given, however, of what this result of investigation was or who gathered it. It is not clear whether the information is of a general nature or is the result of inves-

tigations into Mr Lal's particular case, which clearly differs substantially from that of other Indo-Fijians. It seems the Home Office has made its decisions about this case on the basis of assertions which are based on secret information and which are therefore by their very nature irrefutable and even unexaminable. If Mr Lal is to be given a fair chance, he surely needs to be able to see the evidence against him, to know its provenance and to be given the opportunity to argue against it ... There is a clear and strong case for Mr Lal to be granted refugee status and the Home Office has not yet provided any coherent reasons why this has not been done.

The academic also added a footnote to the Home Secretary, 'Since I gather that papers have gone astray earlier in this affair I venture to include a copy of Mr Victor Lal's side of the dossier'.

The Home Secretary Kenneth Clarke did not bother to reply to the letter. Instead, he announced the reintroduction of the abandoned 1991 Asylum Bill, as the Queen told Parliament in her speech on 6 May outlining the new Tory government's policies: 'A Bill will be presented to enable applications for asylum in the United Kingdom to be determined quickly and effectively.'

In August 1992, I was informed through Asylum Aid that my passport could not be returned to me with an extension of my exceptional leave because my file had been sent from the Home Office to 'another government department' where 'further research' was being conducted on my case. I had no idea when the file was to be brought back to the Home Office and my passport sent out with an extension of my exceptional leave. But what I was sure of was the fact that my case would continue to drag on for a long period of time. The appeal hearing had been set for 17 December 1992 and there was no indication that the Home Office was prepared to back down at the last minute.

On 22 October 1992, the United Kingdom Government published its Asylum and Immigration Appeals Bill. And on 2 November, during the second reading of the Bill in the House of Commons, Kenneth Clarke maintained that

the revised Bill would 'achieve a better system for making prompt and fair decisions' on asylum applications. He also claimed that asylum procedures were being abused by 'economic migrants' who did not qualify as refugees under the 1951 Convention, and that the United Kingdom 'cannot allow anyone to settle ... simply because they come from a country in part of whose territory there is civil war or political strife'. The Bill's stated aims (Dallal Stevens, *International Journal of Refugee Law*, vol. 5, no.1, 1993) were to:
- ensure that the Immigration Rules do not lay down any practice which would be contrary to the 1951 Convention and the Protocol to that Convention (clause 2);
- fingerprint all asylum seekers (clause 3);
- remove the duty upon housing authorities to accommodate asylum seekers and their dependants where they are already occupying accommodation, however temporary (clauses 4 and 5);
- ensure that an asylum seeker is not removed from or required to leave the United Kingdom pending a decision on the asylum claim (clause 6);
- curtail the leave of any person who has permission to be in the UK, for example, a student, who subsequently makes an asylum application which is rejected; on any deportation order, such a person may also be detained (clause 7);
- provide a right to appeal where an asylum claim is rejected (clause 8 and schedule 2);
- extend the liability of airlines and carriers with respect to transit passengers, where a visa restriction has been imposed on the country from which those passengers originate (clause 12).

One of the most important aspects of the Bill, as Dallal Stevens pointed out, was its acceptance that an asylum seeker had a right of oral appeal against refusal of his or her claim. Although the Government had been applauded for its readiness to legislate on the right of appeal, the procedural practicalities of the provisions had been condemned. Cases in which there was no personal delivery of notice must be determined within 42 days of receipt of the notice of appeal by the special adjudicator. In cases involving a refusal of leave to enter where the applicant had been personally served with notice of the refusal of asylum, he or she would have had only two days in which to lodge an appeal. Perhaps of greatest concern was the inclusion of an accelerated procedure in the Bill and in the accompanying Appeals Rules. The Home Secretary was entitled to decide that certain cases were 'without foundation', which automatically imposed a five-day limit on the special adjudicator to determine the appeal. If the adjudicator concurred with the Secretary of State's findings, there was no further right of appeal.

In the meantime, we began preparing for the appeal. Although no oral hearing was initially sought, Asylum Aid by letter dated 27th May 1992, sought a hearing at which 'approximately two witnesses will be called and no interpreters will be required'. We had concluded that the most important things in my favour were the book, the articles and broadcasts – the political reasons for me to fear persecution, as opposed to the racial/religious element. Obviously, the racist nature of the Fiji regime was the ultimate cause of the trouble, but what was likely to get me into particular danger, more than other Indo-Fijians, was the fact that I had been writing, broadcasting and campaigning on the issue.

It was this aspect, therefore, that we decided to pursue most strongly (while, of course, taking into account the more general problems of the treatment of Indo-Fijians). We agreed on the need for absolute clarity and the need to deal with each question in turn, so that the adjudicator (who after all, perhaps knew relatively little about Fiji other than what I was going to tell him) did not get answers to questions mixed up, especially as he takes notes of the proceeding himself.

Meanwhile, in a letter dated 1 July 1992 sent by recorded delivery, the Office of Immigration Appeals informed me, the representatives of the parties, and the office of the

United Nations High Commissioner for Refugees that the appeal would be held on 17 December 1992. Neither the High Commissioner for Refugees nor his Office indicated an intention to be present or represented at the appeal. The two witnesses of mine also declined to testify on my behalf, fearing military reprisals against their families in Fiji.

Nevertheless, on 17 December 1992 I appeared before the Adjudicator at Thanet House on the Strand in London. While Alasadair Mackenzie was representing me, the Home Office was represented by two presenting officers. This particular morning I felt that I was fully prepared to explain and impress upon the adjudicator the merits of my case for political asylum. Moreover, although the room in which the appeal hearing took place had all the trappings of a court house, I felt no sense of uneasiness. During my journalistic career in Fiji I had at one time been the chief crime reporter for *Fiji Sun*, my work taking me from the Magistrates Courts through the Supreme Courts to the Fiji Court of Appeal, mostly dominated by British legal expatriates or British-trained local lawyers. The only visible difference was the fact that, instead of occupying a seat in the press gallery, I was now in the 'dock', explaining myself away to a barrage of questions from Mackenzie and the Home Office representatives, with intermittent interruptions from the adjudicator.

Furthermore, I was no stranger to the world of refugees, having attended most of the seminars on every aspect of the refugee problem, organised by the Refugee Studies Programme at Oxford. Two years previously, in May 1990, I had taken part in a training course on 'The Law of Refugee Status'. The workshop had looked at the five key elements of the Refugee Convention definition of refugee status:

(a) alienage;
(b) genuine risk;
(c) serious harm for which the state is accountable;
(d) nexus to civil or political status; and

(e) the need for and appropriateness of international protection.

Questions addressed at the workshop included the standard of proof in refugee claims; the use of international human rights law to inform refugee determination; the extent of a state's duty to protect its citizens; prosecution as distinguished from persecution; the violation of socioeconomic human rights as the basis for a refugee claim; and the determination of claims grounded in generalised circumstances. At the end of a long gruelling day, Alasdair Mackenzie and I left Thanet House fully satisfied that we had presented a formidable case for political asylum.

On the other hand, one of the Home Office presenting officers, who had maintained a stony distance and an intimidating posture towards me, concluded his submission claiming that:

> 'while it was conceded that in the event of his return to Fiji, the Appellant might suffer some persecution or even harassment, that would be merely of a general kind rather than aimed at him personally and it would fall far short of the Appellant being persecuted.'

The New Year began on a high note of tension and anxiety but I had already greeted the previous five in a similar mood, despite the optimistic (mostly intoxicated) New Year's Eve revellers (especially African friends and sympathisers) toasting to the chant, 'Next Year in Jerusalem', and dancing to the strain of 'Free-ee Nel-son Man-dela' music in the background. I, however, tried to find solace in Bob Marley's 'Exodus', 'Redemption' and above all, 'Get Up, Stand Up For Your Rights – Don't Give Up the Fight'. This New Year however had special immediacy, for I was eagerly awaiting the Adjudicator's judgement.

Two months later, on 12 February 1993, the Adjudicator turned down my appeal under the Immigration Act 1971 Section 19 (1) for political asylum. He refused my application on the grounds that he (i.e. the adjudicator) was not satisfied that my fear of persecution in Fiji was well-founded within the terms of the 1951 United Nations' Convention relating to the Status of Refugees. The Adjudicator however recalled Asylum Aid's submissions on my behalf before him:

> It was not in dispute that the military government had been intolerant so that there had been arrests and torture between May 1987 and 1988, continuing at a reduced level until 1990.
>
> There had been the new racist Constitution in 1990 which had led to the kidnapping of Dr Anirudh Singh, chairman of the Group Against Racial Discrimination in Fiji, and which coincided with the Secretary of State's decision now under review.
>
> The Appellant's book [*Fiji: Coups in Paradise*], which has been produced was a seditious document and since the Opposition had been effectively silenced, the Appellant's fears were well-founded.
>
> Those fears were supported by documents, not least by Mr X's letter and that of Professor Z at Oxford. (I have withheld the names of the letter writers).
>
> The Appellant's fears amounted to discrimination within paragraph 54 and 55 of the handbook on procedures and criteria for examining refugee status which had been issued by the United Nations High Commissioner for Refugees.
>
> This Appellant had a real feeling of apprehension of persecution and physical violence, the latter as suffered by Dr Singh who had burned the post-coup racist Constitution of Fiji.
>
> There was also the risk that this Appellant would be prosecuted on a charge of sedition in respect of his book. [This had happened to others. We also said I would be one of very few people still vocally opposing the regime.]

In his judgement, the Adjudicator noted that 'the burden of proof in these cases is upon the Appellant but to the lower standard required in political asylum cases, so that he has to show a well-founded fear of persecution. That means simply that he had to demonstrate that there would be a reasonable degree of likelihood that he would be persecuted for a reason contrary to the 1951 Convention and 1967 Protocol relating to the Status of Refugees'.

He further observed that the Secretary of State's decision was based upon the view that, since the Appellant's fears did not amount to persecution, he would encounter in Fiji nothing worse than discrimination in employment.

The Adjudicator considered 'carefully' the oral and documentary evidence and the submissions which had been made, noting that:

> It is not in issue that the Appellant is and was a Fijian figure of some prominence, an academic with a journalistic background, a political researcher and an author of a published book *Fiji: Coups in Paradise* which had been published in 1990.

He, however, ruled as follows:

> No doubt, the academic authors of various letters are benevolent and distinguished in their own fields, but their contributions on behalf of the Appellant seemed to be based on information of which he had been the self-serving source.

> Mr X's letter suggests that a number of people greeted the Appellant's disclosures with 'anger and revulsion' and that they would resort to 'whatever means they have at their disposal' in the event of the Appellant's return to Fiji. However, the means at their actual disposal are not clear [Mr X had claimed in his letter to the Home Office: 'The publication of his [Lal's] book, which I have read, and his outright condemnations and commentaries on the two coups in 1987 makes him an extremely vulnerable target of persecution, especially when the coup leader, Brigadier-General Sitiveni Rabuka, has become Deputy Prime Minister and Minister for Home Affairs ... I must

admit that Lal's exposure of the roles played by some of the original coup plotters, many now holding Cabinet, bureaucratic and influential jobs, has been greeted with anger and revulsion, and I have no doubt that they [including the military] would resort to whatever means they have at their disposal against Lal should he return to Fiji.']

The Appellant acknowledged that he was not unaware of the risks which he undertook as an apparently fearless, investigative journalist who achieved high profile in Fiji.

The Appellant has, no doubt, enhanced both his status as well as his political profile by his talks and interviews, including those on the radio, as well as his book *Fiji: Coups in Paradise*. [Publish and be 'hanged' syndrome]

Taken as a whole, the documentary as well as the extensive evidence of the hearing did not support the Appellant's case that he feared persecution as defined, or even that he would be prosecuted in the event of his return to Fiji.

The evidence had suggested that if he were to be prosecuted, the proceedings would be fair. However, the Appellant's high profile as presented makes either of those risks seem unlikely. [A long-standing supporter of mine later wrote in a humorous strain to a Tory minister: 'Screams of laughter if it were a Monty Python film!'].

The Appellant was not a credible witness in respect of the reality of his personal fears.

The Appellant has not discharged the burden of proof which I have described and the Respondent's (Secretary of State) decision accorded with domestic and international law.

The Appeal is dismissed under the Immigration Act 1971 section 19(1) (b).

The Adjudicator's determination was extremely annoying, to put it mildly. He appeared to think that a person who (like me) openly criticized a regime more or less deserved what he got, or at least did not deserve protection. The good news, however, was that the determination was full of holes: the Adjudicator at various points contradicted himself, failed to support his arguments, ignored vital evidence, and made wildly unsubstantiated remarks about the credibility of the Oxford academics and the former coup plotter's letters of support. Therefore Alasdair Mackenzie and I felt that we had ample grounds for appealing against the refusal, and we thought I stood a strong chance of getting the case heard by the Immigration Appeals Tribunal, on the grounds of the Adjudicator's 'irrationality and failure to consider the evidence'. Furthermore, the judgement failed to take into account the modern concept of 'refugee' in international law.

I was also heartened by the knowledge that two high-ranking Oxford academics, the former coup plotter and Fijian Cabinet Minister Mr X, Dr Singh, the chairman of the Group Against Racial Discrimination in Fiji, and Don Dunstan, a member of the International Commission of Jurists (Australia section) and president of the Movement for Democracy and Human Rights in Fiji, had all agreed to testify on my behalf at the Immigration Appeals Tribunal.

In February, I lodged an appeal with the Immigration Appeals Tribunal against the decision of the Adjudicator. Alasdair Mackenzie submitted voluminous grounds in support of my application for leave to appeal. Grounds of appeal to the Tribunal were as follows:

> The Adjudicator has omitted or misunderstood much important evidence, including both evidence given orally and written evidence. On at least one aspect of the evidence, his treatment of it is contradictory.

> The Adjudicator has come to incorrect and apparently unsubstantiated conclusions about the situation in Fiji and about the credibility of some of the written evidence submitted in the Appellant's favour.

The Adjudicator's apparent implication that the Appellant's political activities are self-serving, and therefore to be discounted in respect of his asylum claim, is incorrect and unsubstantiated.

The Adjudicator has failed to address the question of what constitutes persecution, and in particular of whether the Secretary of State's apparent acceptance of the threat of severe discrimination against the Appellant amounts to an acceptance of the threat of persecution.

The Adjudicator gives no reasonable ground for not believing the Appellant's fear of persecution to be a creditable fear.

It is submitted that had the Adjudicator correctly and reasonably interpreted the evidence before him, he would not have dismissed the appeal. On a proper understanding of the evidence, the Appellant's fear of being persecuted in Fiji is well-founded.

On 28 April 1993 I received a letter informing me that my appeal to the Immigration Appeals Tribunal had been fixed for 11th May, but it was unlikely that I would be called to give evidence. At the brief hearing, the Tribunal admitted my grounds of appeal and that the Adjudicator had got his facts wrong, had omitted to take into account, and had misunderstood, both oral and documentary evidence, and had omitted to record parts of the evidence. The Tribunal noted that:

> As it appears that the Adjudicator had misunderstood some of the evidence before him, there must be at least some doubt as to whether that did not affect his views of the appellant. [Also,] although the Adjudicator was entitled to make assessments of an appellant's credibility, for these to have any meaning he should have provided reasons for his belief. In this case he had failed to do so.

It was surprising that the Adjudicator had done this, but not that the Tribunal criticised him for doing so. Of greater importance and interest was the concern expressed by the chairman of the Tribunal that:

> The Adjudicator has written his comments on the document which contained the appellant's grounds of appeal. With respect, in our view, an adjudicator should restrain himself from expressing his views on the document itself. [Furthermore] his comments had not been sought in this case.

The Adjudicator's comments, written in red in the margins of my appeal submission, read as follows: 'No! The appellant did not say this!'.

The Tribunal admitted the grounds of appeal but allowed it to the extent that it was remitted for hearing *de novo* by an adjudicator other than Mr Y (Adjudicator's name withheld). The Home Office representative, who had come prepared to proceed with the appeal, initially objected to a remittal on the grounds that a whole day had been set aside for the appeal but subsequently, and after strong objections from Mackenzie, agreed that the Adjudicator appeared to have misunderstood some of the evidence. A new hearing date for appeal was set for 29 October 1993 and later moved forward to 8 November.

As previously, we made further submissions to the Home Office, in the vain hope that with the new legislation on refugees coming in, it might just be that the Home Office would want to cave in on old cases, so as to concentrate on throwing out new ones. This could work to our advantage, if not to the advantage of others.

In asking the Home Office to reconsider its decision, further information consisted of a 1990 report from the International Federation of Journalists (IJF) on press freedom in Fiji, and relevant excerpts from a number of issues of *Fiji Voice*, an independent newsletter published in Australia. Its publisher, Don Dunstan, an acquaintance of mine, is a Fiji-born Australian lawyer, a former Premier and Attorney-General of the state of South Australia. These publications made clear the extent to which the press had been muzzled in Fiji. The 1990 IFJ report particularly stressed the danger of a military crackdown on dissident journalists, of whom I was clearly one. It indicated that the absence of continued arrests of journalists in 1989 and 1990 had more to do with the fact that journalists had either complied with the government's attempts to censor them, or had left the country, than with any increase in official tolerance of dissent.

Don Dunstan later wrote to the British Home Office confirming my fears of persecution in Fiji. In his letter he stated that:

> I know Mr Victor Lal, and am aware of his academic studies on Fiji and its government. He has been strongly critical of the regime and the coups in Fiji, and of senior personalities in the present government. If he returns to Fiji he is in danger at worst of physical violence and at least to severe discrimination in employment. After the second coup Som Prakash (now an academic in Australia but then in Fiji) was arrested, subjected to physical and emotional torture and released under threats as to what would happen to his family if he talked about his experiences. The regime's complaint about him was that he had written an uncomplimentary critique of a book seeking to justify the first coup by Rabuka, the then military dictator and present Prime Minister in the Fiji government. Victor Lal's criticisms of Rabuka and a whole swathe of the Fijian establishment make Prakash's critique mild in the extreme by comparison.

Dunstan also reminded the Home Office that he was 'flown to England at British government expense in March of this year (1993) at the request of the Crown Service to give evidence in the case of R v Laing as to the claim by the accused that he was involved with so-called Fiji Freedom Fighters'.

It was clear, Mackenzie argued, that I was a prominent Fijian dissident whose opinions and actions could not fail to be well-known to the Fijian government. Moreover, I was personally known to a number of the main protagonists in the coup, whom I had criticised openly in my book for their role, and I had written and broadcasted widely on the political situation in Fiji. It was also clear that the junta in Fiji was completely intolerant of criticism. *The Fiji Sun*, which bravely challenged the army the day after the first 1987 coup, was attacked and harassed by the army. After it resumed publication on 21st May 1987, sympathising with the elected Prime Minister Timoci Bavadra, it was faced with mounting censorship and finally closed. This was clearly detailed in both the IFJ report and in the February 1988 issue of *Fiji Voice*.

We also pointed out the mass arrests and torture of government opponents that took place frequently between May 1987 and the end of 1988, and, albeit at a reduced level in 1989 and 1990, as reported by Amnesty International. The new Constitution of Fiji in 1990 entrenched the suppression of Indo-Fijians and it was this that led to the arrest of Dr Singh and others who demonstrated against it. We also enclosed the findings of an Australian parliamentary delegation, led by Dr Andrew Theophanus, to Fiji. He had clearly detailed instances of army brutality against the Indo-Fijians.

It was precisely during this period, when I was writing and broadcasting widely against the Fijian government and in favour of Indo-Fijian rights, that the Secretary of State made his decision to refuse to recognise me as a refugee.

In particular, we had submitted two specific extracts from books by victims of the Fijian military junta to the Home Office. The first book (*The Guns of Lautoka*, 1988) by a Canadian-born, Auckland-based criminal lawyer Christopher Harder, who had gone to Fiji to defend several individuals charged with different offences, contained an account of his own detention in a Fiji military jail, and what he saw and heard during his incarceration. In the book, Harder recalled the beatings of an old acquaintance of mine, Som Prakash, a university lecturer and a chess enthusiast, who had criticised the coup leader's autobiography. According to Harder:

Every time I went to the bathroom I also briefly looked into the next door cell where the inhabitant was stretched out on the corridor floor in a similar position to me. His room seemed darker somehow. Was his window covered or did the cell just not get as much light as mine? At times the atmosphere in the cells was simply a level of dull fear, at times it was electric. One particular security force interrogator similarly tattooed to the rest had a terrible questioning technique. He made the Indian in the cell come to the bar and, in a most harsh voice, yelled, 'I am only going to ask you this question once, I am a busy man. I haven't got time to waste. So you think when you answer it and you tell me'.

He asked the Indian if he had discussed the Brigadier (the coup leader who had promoted himself to that rank) over lunch. The Indian stuttered and said 'No' in a voice twinged with fear and concern. 'You are wrong, you lie. You are under the decree. If you don't tell the truth, you will be shot'. 'But that's the truth, that's truth. I not talk about, I not talk about Rabuka...'. But locked away in my tiny cell there was nothing I could do as this psychological interrogation went on around me.

A fellow human being was being subjected to extreme mental torment, having no idea how long he was going to be there, why he was really there, whether he would be charged or jailed or shot or beaten: these were all real possibilities for the Indian.

The Indians were divided. They were separated. They were all but naked. They were being treated no better than dogs and feared for their lives. I watched as the lecturer from the university, Som Prakash, who had written the critique on the Rabuka book *No Other Way*, was marched past my cell, returning obviously from the toilet. He was barefooted wearing blue, typically Indian pyjama pants and no top; a chubby man with a bit of a bulge for his probably 40 or 42 years of age. Yet he had a look of independence, a look of pride.

As he walked by I was reminded of the film *Gandhi* and the scenes where he would continue to turn the other cheek and not be scared of the pain. He was a brave man.

I later heard him being yelled at on Thursday morning, as a guard stormed down between the cells with a metal rod in his hand. It was about three feet long, little more than a piece of thick wire with a sliding metal cap on one end. As he walked past my cell towards the professor's he yelled for another guard, 'Open the gate. Quickly, quickly open it, open it!'

The second guard dropped the keys in his rush. They unlocked the cell and went in. 'Thwack, thwack' I heard twice. The only conclusion I could fairly draw was that he had gone in and beaten the lecturer with the rod because I heard him cry out with pain but not utter a coherent word. They relocked his cell and the security man walked off into the main office.

Paradoxically Som Prakash, who was detained and tortured twice by the military, even faced mindless animosity from highly educated ethnic Fijians. At a meeting of senior school teachers and academics it was reported that:

> Ethnic Fijian school teachers became so hostile when they learned of his presence in the meeting that some rose to attack him physically – this harassment shows clearly how little even some educated Fijians understand the concepts of democracy and individual human rights, and how the simple ideals of culture and tradition still dominate their lifestyle.

Sadly, a former ethnic Fijian journalist colleague of mine had hastily joined the military's revamped Ministry of Information and became its chief propagandist – the Goebbels of Fiji – against the Indo-Fijians and the military critics at home and abroad.

Other grim stories of torture, rape, and harassment of Indo-Fijians by Fijian soldiers and their supporters followed and were later corroborated by Amnesty International. The Indo-Fijians were beaten, forced to stand in sewage pools, and subjected to other forms of humiliating treatment.

In the case of Dr Singh, a lecturer in physics at the University of the South Pacific (USP) in Fiji, we sent to the Home Office an extract from his book *Silent Warriors* (April 1991). Dr Singh was abducted from outside his home on 24 October 1990, bundled into a car and driven off to a secluded woodland in Fiji. He had bandages taped over his eyes and a hood tied down tight over his head. He was repeatedly beaten and interrogated about his fellow protesters, and about his contacts in Australia and London. They also retrieved a list of names and phone numbers that he always kept with him for ready reference. At one point his hands were smashed against a root with a metal pipe and they also forcibly cut his hair and burnt him with cigarettes. But before they left, one of his captors lit a match and began burning the already-cut hair at the tips, some kind of pagan ceremony of humiliation. The whole ordeal lasted for eleven hours. Dr Singh was finally set free, and had lived to tell his tale.

Who was behind the abduction, and why was it carried out? Six days after Dr Singh's abduction, five members of the Royal Fiji Military Forces including a captain and four corporals gave themselves up as responsible. Although the abduction was led by Captain Sotia Ponijiasi, who served with Britain's elite Special Air Services (SAS) during the 1960s, it was a much wider conspiracy involving the army, the police and members of the Fijian regime. The abduction, Dr Singh later claimed, was clearly an act of state-organised terrorism, intended to implant fear in the regime's opponents and to deter further overt demonstrations against the new racist Constitution. The regime realised this objective fully. The abduction generated mass petrification amongst a community which had already been in a state of fear.

Worse still, the trial of Dr Singh's abductors that followed was clearly biased heavily in favour of the abductors, and was a sad indictment on the state of independence and impartiality of the judiciary in Fiji. The five were given a 12-month prison sentence (suspended for 15 months), and a fine of $F345 per accused, which Dr Singh protested as 'a ludicrously lenient sentence by any standards'. One of the abductors was later dispatched to Kuwait as a 'peacekeeper' and was only sent back to Fiji by the UN after an international outcry against his posting. A human rights group had recognised Captain Ponijiasi in the departure ceremony in Fiji.

In mitigation, the military abductors had claimed in court that they had reacted in a brutal manner towards Dr Singh because of the perceived insult to the traditional Fijian chiefs. They were acting within the bounds of the new Constitution, specifically Section 100, which gives ethnic Fijian Customary Laws an overriding applicability in Fiji to everyone (regardless of one's own customs and traditions). The abductors defence counsel referred to Section 100, and successfully claimed that the abductors 'were provoked in doing what they did to the complainant [Dr Singh] whom they considered to have insulted the President [Ratu Ganilau], the Prime Minister [Ratu Mara] and the members of the Great Council of Chiefs and the Fijian people generally, when he took part in the burning of the Constitution as reported in the news media'.

To add insult to injury, and perhaps as a warning to opponents of racism and military rule, Dr Singh, when finally discharged from hospital on 15 November 1990, was immediately released into the waiting hands of the police. They took him to the capital's Central Police Station where he was formally charged with sedition – for burning the racist new Constitution of Fiji. In fact, shortly after the coup in 1987, the military, through its reconstituted Ministry of Information (in fact Misinformation) had issued an international press statement warning the critics of the regime, both in Fiji and abroad, that they would face prosecution if they 'spread false information' about the situation in Fiji. According to the former coup plotter Mr X, I was already on the top of their overseas lists of 'wanted persons'. The military, according to him, had been monitoring my BBC World Service broadcasts, and the Fijian embassy in London had been supplementing other missing details about TV interviews, newspaper articles, and lectures conducted by me.

In passing, it may be worth mentioning that my book *Fiji: Coups in Paradise*, contains the most vicious but frank attack on the traditional Great Council of Chiefs. It systematically exposes the conspiratorial roles, both before and after the coup, of Ratu Mara, Ratu Ganilau and other political Fijian high chiefs, and clearly violates Section 100. It therefore makes me the foremost candidate for prosecution and persecution in Fiji, even though I ended the book on a pleading note:

> But the chiefs determined to imprison themselves in the racist garb of supremacy and tradition, and their antagonists, the Fijian Indians, threatening violence and vengeance, both sides must be urged to re-examine the findings of the Royal Commission that investigated Fiji's electoral system in 1975. This Commission had strongly advocated the extending of national seats in order to defeat the politics of communalism. The chiefs, prejudiced by lack of vision, must, on the other hand, in the months and years to come, and in order to save their country from the calamity that confronts them, realise that 'tradition is a guide, not a jailer'; the Fiji Indians with a history of rebellion on the sugar plantations and burning political ambitions in their hearts are repeating the lines of Richard Lovelace: 'Stone walls do not a prison make – Nor iron bars a cage'.

The above statement/plea was made neither in haste nor rage. Its roots lie deep in my own personal and family history. If I may say so with humility (and shame), ours was a family whose political loyalty and fortune was tied to that of the ruling Fijian chiefs and their supposedly multi-racial Alliance Party. For several years my father, an Indo-Fijian (also fluent in several native Fijian dialects), was chairman of the Alliance Party in the rural district of Tailevu. He had successfully campaigned on behalf of several Fijian MPs, especially two high Fijian chiefs (the late Ratu George Cakobau and Ratu Penaia Ganilau) who went on to become Governors-general of post-independent Fiji. Many times he humbly sat and (according to Fijian custom) made me sit at the feet of the High Chief and Prime Minister Ratu Mara during election campaigns or at the Prime Minister's residence in the capital Suva. My father's brother also served as an Alliance mayor of Suva, despite strong objections from the Indo-Fijian population, mostly supporters of the oppositional National Federation Party. We strongly and genuinely believed in the Alliance Party's pre-coup 'politics of multi-racialism'.

On my part, I was among the first group of Indo-Fijians to be educated in an elite all indigenous Fijian school, until then considered the bastion of the Fijian chiefly, political, military, and administrative establishment. Many of its indigenous Fijian former pupils went on to assume the leadership of the country, and are still running or representing Fiji under the premiership of coup leader Rabuka. For example my former mathematics teacher is (at the time of writing) Permanent Secretary for Foreign Affairs. Others associated with the school included my principal, who became Fiji's Ambassador to New Zealand, a former Director of Public Prosecutions (who was a teacher at the school), racist Methodist Church leaders, University lecturers and professors, lawyers, and several army officers. These latter included the Commander of the Army, Ratu Mara's son-in-law and a former close personal friend of mine, who was deposed in the coup but later appointed Fiji's Ambassador to Great Britain.

I had been wrenched away from my family and sent to the elite Fijian school, 'to fulfil Ratu Mara's politics of multi-racialism' as my father had put it to me. Until then, I had been planning to attend the Mahatma Gandhi Memorial School in Fiji, established in memory of the great Indian nationalist leader. In the early years, my father greatly admired the Indian nationalist leaders and even went to the extent of adding 'Lal' as my surname, in emulation of Pandit Jawaharlal Nehru, the first Prime Minister of modern India. He used to constantly remind us of Nehru's role in the struggle for the freedom of our indentured forebears in Fiji and elsewhere in the British colonies, and, more importantly, of Nehru's plea that 'integration' was the key to overseas Indians' survival in foreign lands. Nehru had raised the issue of citizenship, including that of Indo-Fijians, in the Lok Sabha on 8 March 1948:

> Now these Indians abroad ... Are they Indian citizens ... or not? If not, then our interest in them becomes cultural and humanitarian, not political ... Take the Indians of Fiji or Mauritius: are they going to retain their nationality, or will they become Fiji nationals or Mauritians ... This House wants to treat them as Indians, and with the same breath it wants a complete franchise for them in the countries they are living. Of course, the two things do not go together. Either they get the franchise as nationals of the country, or treat them as Indians minus the franchise and ask for them the most favourable treatment.

For my father, a chauvinistically devout Hindu who prayed twice a day, Fiji's future lay in the intermingling of the races in the schools, and in our satchels we were supposed to carry the multi-racial future of Fiji. I was expected to play a constructive role in that future – political or otherwise. I, however, chose to enter the field of journalism, hoping to act as a 'night watchman' of the nation. As a journalist, I also began to cast doubt on my father's fanatical faith in Ratu Mara's 'politics of multi-racialism', and later exposed Mara's politics as a sham, first in the 1982 general elections, later in the 1987 elections, and especially his conspiratorial roles before and after the coup. He became Prime Minister in Rabuka's military government and is now the President of Fiji, defending his shift from the 'politics of multi-racialism' to the 'politics of racism' as follows:

> We cannot go back to the [1970] Fiji Constitution in which we enjoyed peace and stability for a long time and we have to find a Constitution that has to accommodate what has now been shown quite clearly: the wish of the indigenous people.

The solution was found in the promulgation of the racist 1990 Constitution of Fiji, which the International Commission of Jurists described as 'quite as bad' as the apartheid laws in South Africa. The jurists concluded:

> The government will not be answerable to the governed. Racial and geographical divisions and discrimination against citizens of all races are enshrined in the Constitution which the majority is powerless to alter.

Although the Constitution has the 'trappings' of representative government, the jurists say, it lacks the 'reality'. I do not know my father's reaction to the new racist Constitution, for 'dead men tell no tales'. I am however sure that my late father would have condemned it as a sorry tale of 'great betrayal' and would have urged me to do likewise. The plea to the traditional Fijian high chiefs, in a way, is a plea on behalf of my father's vision of a genuinely multi-racial Fiji.

My own crusade against Fijian racism is therefore deeply rooted, and in part, influenced by Ratu Mara's previous preaching of the 'politics of multi-racialism'. In other words, to paraphrase the former white South African editor Donald Woods who made international headlines in 1977 when under threat of death he fled his country to Great Britain, I had not emerged on the international scene a decade later, 'asking for trouble'. I genuinely believed (and still do) that Fiji belongs to all who live in it, and that no government, especially a military-inspired racist government, can justly claim authority unless it is based on the will of all the people of Fiji.

Furthermore I strongly resented, on the basis of my political and personal background, the general Fijian portrayal of the Indo-Fijians as 'mean and stingy, crafty and demanding to the extent of being considered greedy, inconsiderate and grasping, uncooperative, egotistic, and calculating'. These assertions are made by one of the former pupils of the previously mentioned elite school. The author, a Fijian professor in Pacific studies, had in 1988 shamelessly made similar allegations against the Indo-

Fijians at the British Foreign and Commonwealth Office Research Department seminar on Fiji in London, but which I then had an opportunity to rebut from across the table.

In 1991, he repeated the charges in his book *The Facade of Democracy*, which was hailed by the former Governor-General and President of post-coup Fiji, the late Ratu Ganilau, as the first Fijian response to the 'barrage of book-length criticism' delivered to Fijians since 1987. This 'barrage' he said, came from 'numerous journalists and academics' aboard a 'bandwagon of invective' and by 'dilettantes' masquerading as experts. He condemned most of the post-coup books, by one count about fifteen, including *Fiji: Coups in Paradise – Race, Politics and Military Intervention*, in which I had predicted the coup and had condemned its subsequent racist aftermath.

While launching the professor's book on 16 June 1991, the President of Fiji claimed that *Facade of Democracy* was a response entirely within the Fijian character: measured, positive, optimistic and seeking to put events in their proper historical context. The President deliberately chose to ignore the historical and political connection of my family to him, the Alliance Party, and the traditional Fijian high chiefs. In a similar vein, the Home Office and the Adjudicator refused to take into consideration this aspect of our submission for political asylum. In other words, I was both an outsider and an insider in the inner sanctums of Fijian culture and politics. The Fijian establishment had tried to kill my message of multi-racialism and was prepared to kill the messenger, and so we argued in all our submissions for political asylum in Great Britain.

The other obnoxious aspect of the new Fijian Customary Laws relates to death. In a murder trial, two ethnic Fijians who had murdered an Indo-Fijian farmer, quoted in mitigation that they had performed a *sevu sevu* – an act of forgiveness – on the murdered farmer's family. According to ethnic Fijian custom, the acceptance of such a ceremony automatically means a granting of forgiveness. It could be correctly inferred therefore that the family of political opponents – in the eventuality of a 'political death'– cannot rely on the Fijian state for justice. Moreover, it seems that Dr Singh's brutal abductors had presumably forgotten this aspect of the law of forgiveness during the eleven hours of their barbaric mission, which Dr Singh had concluded would end in his death.

I had first established contact with Dr Singh when he phoned me from somewhere in England in 1987 after seeing me on British television and having read my articles on the coup in newspapers. His voice was cracking with a burning desire to do something about the racial situation in Fiji, a desire which later found expression in the founding of the Group Against Racial Discrimination as well as the public burning of the new 1990 Constitution of Fiji. I had also been in contact with several imprisoned members of the overthrown Coalition government, human and political rights activists, and pro-democracy movement supporters in Fiji . Hence, Alasdair Mackenzie stressed that:

> It may be argued that the treatment of Dr Singh is not typical, but dissent on the scale that he attempted it, and on the scale that Mr Lal has exhibited it, is by necessity rare in Fiji. What the enclosed reports make clear is the extent to which dissent within the country has evaporated because of the continued threat of military action. It is apparent, though, that when individuals have attempted to express their opposition to the regime even in a peaceful manner, they have been charged with sedition or public offences, and, in the case of Anirudh Singh, attacked and tortured in an appalling manner.

He added that:

> It would appear reasonable for Mr Lal to believe that he too would be at risk of attack, and that the government would be unwilling or unable to defend him. He also fears, quite reasonably, that the government will press charges against him. His activities against the Fijian regime are far more public, far more sustained and far more fundamental than Dr Singh's. If burning the constitution, as Dr Singh did, is considered seditious, then Mr

Lal's book, which so openly and unambiguously attacks the Fijian government and its leaders, is much more seditious. ... In fact, I would suggest also that there is a very real danger of physical violence being meted out to Mr Lal, as in the case of Dr Singh, and many other detainees since the coup, and also there is a very serious danger of legal proceedings being taken against him on charges of sedition or similar charges, with the accompanying risk to his liberty. These latter risks would without doubt amount to persecution.

During the interval between hearings, the Home Office, however, phoned Asylum Aid to say that they were still reconsidering the evidence I had put in about my claim. Therefore they would be asking for an adjournment of the appeal hearing on 8th November. This would have to be agreed by the Adjudicator, of course. Obviously, this was a good sign, as it presumably meant they were taking my evidence seriously.

At this point, I decided to involve a Conservative Cabinet Minister as well as Dr Barbara Harrell-Bond, the Director of the Oxford Refugee Studies Programme, on my case. It proved decisive and the whole case suddenly took a new twist. I also reminded the Home Office that they still held my Fijian passport (which was still valid until 28 August 1994 but dangerous to use), and had to renew my exceptional leave to remain, pending a decision on my claim for refugee status. My passport was returned at last, with a visa allowing me to stay for a further three years. The Home Office was still considering my application for refugee status.

In September 1993, a letter was brought to my attention from Sakeasi Butadroka, an ultra-racist Fijian leader, to the British Prime Minister, John Major. The letter, written on 19 October 1992, called on Britain to be held responsible for the welfare of Fiji's Indo-Fijian community and thereby fulfil its Deed of Cession obligations to the indigenous people of Fiji. The veteran nationalist also called on John Major to make British passports available to people from Fiji, and said that he wanted to see Fiji ruled by an exclusively Fijian Parliament with the Senate replaced by the Great Council of Chiefs.

I immediately wrote to John Major seeking clarification. On 21 September, the British Foreign and Commonwealth Office's (FCO) South Pacific Department replied on behalf of the Prime Minister, and enclosed a copy of a press release issued by the British Embassy in Suva on 12 November 1992 which indicated the terms of the reply sent to Butadroka's letter. The FCO also assured me that, 'we continue to follow closely events as they unfold in Fiji including the review of the Constitution which is now underway'.

In his reply to Butadroka's letter to the Prime Minister, the latter's private Secretary said that the British Government rejected the historical claim in Butadroka's letter. Moreover, 'it would not be appropriate for the British Government to intervene in Fiji's internal affairs in the way in which Mr Butadroka had suggested'.

In April 1988, Butadroka had written a similar letter to the late Indian Prime Minister Rajiv Gandhi urging him to ship Indo-Fijians from Fiji because they did not have any political future in Fiji. Butadroka and his threat of actions could not be dismissed lightly. A former assistant Cabinet Minister, he was jailed in the 1970s for his extreme racist views. In 1975 he had tabled a motion in Parliament calling for the expulsion of Indo-Fijians in the style of President Idi Amin of Uganda. In 1977, Butadroka and his Fijian Nationalist Party did not rule out using violence to achieve their aim of 'driving Indians into the sea'. He later became a Minister in the short-lived post-military coup government. I had dealt with him in my capacity as a journalist, and knew his power for mischief and extremism far better than the FCO officials and other so-called experts on Fiji. A journalist colleague of mine had become a victim of his supporters' violence in the aftermath of the coup, suffering a broken arm. His Fiji nationality was later revoked and he was given 28 days to leave the country. In short, the ultra-nationalist racist was a man of words as well as violent action.

In late October 1993, Asylum Aid notified me that the appeal hearing for 8 November had been cancelled, and that the Home Office had asked for at least six months to consider the evidence I had submitted. The ordeal of asylum was now in its fifth year, a further six months meant I would know about my fate sometime in April 1994 (maybe).

The long and unpredictable ordeal also intruded into two other issues. Firstly, my long-standing Norwegian fiancée (now my wife) and I had agreed since our first meeting in Oxford in 1988 that we should get married in 1993; secondly, in late November I learnt that the Norwegian Nobel Institute in Oslo had granted me a Guest Nobel Fellowship to research the history of the Nobel Peace Prize for my forthcoming book. I was suddenly presented with multiple dilemmas: marriage, travel, fellowship, and even residency.

The matter of residency was really very complicated. I could try and get residency in both Norway and the United Kingdom, but this would be virtually impossible. On the other hand, I could not pursue my application for refugee status in the UK if I moved permanently to Norway. If I did get refugee status in the UK before going to Norway, I did not see why this need affect my residency, or even my eventual citizenship in Norway. Citizenship would simply supersede my need for UN protection (i.e. for refugee status). I would lose my refugee status and therefore my residency in the UK, but, of course, this would not prevent me returning to the UK at a later date for personal or academic reasons.

If I had refugee status I could, of course, use a UN Travel Document. With exceptional leave, which is what I had then, I would be expected to apply to the Fijian embassy (since the coup to the authorities in Fiji) to renew my passport. If they turned that down, I could apply to the Home Office for a travel document, but this could take up to six months and there would be no guarantee of success and, in fact, I had already been turned down once.

If I decided to go to Norway, I would need to check on my rights to stay there without a valid passport, and to see if the Norwegians would issue me with a travel document if I could not get a passport. They might let me stay there regardless, or I could, of course, apply for asylum there as a last resort. The last idea was totally out of question, for I already had a bitter taste of waiting for a decision in England. The so-called 'refugee problem' in Norway, according to press cuttings, was no different from that in the United Kingdom, if not in numbers, then certainly in approach. In the end I decided to use my Fiji passport, which expired on 28 August 1994, and which contained exceptional leave to remain in the United Kingdom. In fact, the Home Office advised me that I was not entitled to a travel document as long as I had a valid passport, especially as I had exceptional leave to remain in the United Kingdom. I allowed fate to take its natural course.

In Norway, although I had a very interesting time at the Nobel Institute (apart from the theft of my wallet and the Fiji passport, which I later found), my brush with the authorities was of a fairly difficult nature. An day before our planned marriage on 7 January 1994 (still etched on our wedding rings), the officer at the Marriage Registry called me in to inform me that she could not sanction my marriage, for I had to produce letters of proof from the Fiji government of my past marital status; she had clearly mistaken me for an Englishman (Victor is, after all, a very European name). My problem with the Fijian authorities was not her problem. What about the wedding food and the guests? That was not her problem either.

At that moment I felt that the world was a terribly cold and cruel place, especially for a person in exile, for 'exile is the xenophobe – for every single one who likes you, you'll find ten in whom there is nothing but hate'. Those in exile are penalised for trying to rebuild their shattered lives, but it seems that those holding sway over their fate are not penalised for making official and unpardonable mistakes. For my wife-to-be, the only consolation were the following words: 'Till Laws – Do Us Part'.

Notes

1. Jacqueline Bhabha and Sue Shutter, *Women's Movement – Women under immigration, nationality and refugee law*, Trentham Books, London, 1994.

2. Quoted in John Lester and Pierre Spoerri, *Rediscovering Freedom*, Grosvenor Books, London, 1992.

3. Richard Dunstan, *Amnesty International Bulletin*, October/November 1991. See also Dunstan, *Amnesty International Bulletin*, April/May 1992.

From Reporter to Refugee

A 'Babylonian World'

Amidst the dark gloom in Norway – the Land of the Midnight Sun – there was finally a ray of light. On 3 February 1994, Alasdair Mackenzie informed me that the Home Office had, at long last, changed its mind and decided to recognise me as a refugee. The message was conveyed by the Home Office Minister responsible for immigration to the Tory Cabinet Minister handling my case. Mackenzie's note added, 'I suppose this just shows that persistence can pay off!'. Indeed, but how many refugees have the patience to pursue their cases and the access to those in power which I enjoyed? Or, as in my case, the untiring support and determination of Alasdair Mackenzie?

In his letter to the Tory minister dated 27 January 1994, the Home Office Minister noted:

> Having carefully considered the contents of Mr Mackenzie's letter together with the other additional information which he had submitted on behalf of Mr Lal since the application was originally refused, we have concluded that the original decision should be reversed and we shall recognise Mr Lal as a refugee under the terms of the 1951 United Nations' Convention.

The specialist Asylum Division of the Immigration and Nationality Department was to write to Mackenzie separately in due course confirming that I had been recognised as a refugee and inviting me to withdraw my appeal against the original decision.

Seven years after I made my original claim, I was finally granted Refugee Status under the United Nations Convention Relating to the Status of Refugees of 28 July 1951 and its Protocol of 1967.

By March 1994 it was time to leave Norway for England, to collect my papers, and to apply for a United Nations Travel Document. My planned marriage had collapsed (in fact, the Norwegians had refused to sanction it) and my three-month visa in Norway had run out. On 20 March I returned to Oxford and had to camp at a friend's house. Some other asylum seekers were not as fortunate as me. The atmosphere in Oxford also seemed to have changed. The government had transformed Campsfield House, a complex near Oxford which had previously been used as a prison, into a holding centre for asylum seekers. I also learnt that since 11 March, at least 135 of the 200 'inmates' were on hunger strike.

The next month I read screaming headlines in the newspapers: 'Home Office Unmoved by Hunger Strikers.' Interestingly, the very Minister responsible for reversing my rejected application for asylum, was informing Parliament that less than 5 per cent of today's asylum seekers met the 1951 Geneva Convention criterion of having 'a wellfounded fear of persecution'. At that time, there were some 47,000 would-be refugees in Britain, of whom 645 were in detention, most having had their applications to stay rejected.

He also insisted that he would not be 'blackmailed' by asylum seekers going on hunger strike. According to him, the Government had not been helped in its ability to handle the hunger strikers in a measured way because of the 'hysterical and at times aggressive behaviour of the rent-a-mob crowd' who frequently gathered outside Campsfield House. He claimed that

> It has been a motley crowd of the Oxford Trades Union Council, the Socialist Workers' Party, the Revolutionary Communist Party and others of that ilk.

I was among the so-called 'rent-a-mob' crowd but was certainly not a member of any of the above-mentioned organisations. I was there in my capacity as a newly declared refugee who, even if I did not know the facts of the cases, at least understood the anguish and clamour for freedom asylum seekers experience. I kept asking myself one simple question: was the fate of these asylum seekers determined after seven long gruelling years, seven months, seven weeks or even seven seconds? Was the same Adjudicator, who had wrongly determined my case, now responsible for keeping one of these asylum seekers behind the barbed-wire fences at Campsfield House in Oxford? Although he would not have put them there, he might easily have refused to release one on bail.

In July, I read another article entitled 'Study undermined popular conceptions of refugees' in *The Guardian*. The paper disclosed that among the research projects shelved by Home Office ministers was one on refugees, which the minister responsible for immigration refused to publish. Results showed that half the sample of refugees interviewed had to wait 16 months or more for a decision on their case by the Immigration and Nationality Department. More than a fifth were kept waiting for 30 months or more, with one case waiting nearly six years. As a matter of fact, I was not among those interviewed so the fact that I had waited for seven long and bruising years did not go on record in this document.

It is also worth noting that, along with the problem of asylum seekers, MPs had also raised the fear among refugees from past decades of a resurgence of anti-Semitism. One Tory MP told the House:

> Many of my constituents were refugees from the Nazis. They fought for Britain in the last war and they see in the evening of their lives a chilling echo of the 1930s.

Cemeteries had been daubed with anti-Semitic slogans and Nazi emblems, and synagogues and schools had to have security staff to guard against thugs. The MP added:

'It is surely a position that in the last years of the 20th century places of worship should need to be protected' (*The Independent*).

The Tory MP, Sir Ivan Lawrence, himself a Jew, said he did not believe that the Government appreciated the extent to which racism was increasing or the fear it caused. He said:

> With the rise of extremist organisations in Europe and, inevitably, to some extent in Britain, it is time to build up our defences against the cancer of racism brought home to us so powerfully in the film *Schindler's List*.

But the Fijian brand of racism, compared by a native Fijian church minister to Hitler's Nazism in Germany, seemed to be of no concern to the Tory government of the day, even though the Indo-Fijians' (contemptuously referred to as the 'Brown Jews of Fiji') homes and their places of worship had been looted and vandalised, and a strict fundamentalist Methodism enforced. The coup leader and current Prime Minister Sitiveni Rabuka believes that Indo-Fijians, whom he describes as heathens, must be converted to Christianity 'or they convert us and we all become heathens'.

The BBC's own documentary programme *Paradise in Peril*, a graphic and chilling account of racism and terror in Fiji, failed to evoke the same response as *Schindler's List*. My own long list of the grounds for political asylum had no effect on the Home Secretaries who presided over my case. Perhaps the *Daily Telegraph*, a newspaper sympathetic to the Tory establishment, spoke on behalf of the vociferous minority. In an editorial entitled 'Inverted Racism', it asked on 28 May 1987:

> Why has there been no call for sanctions against Fiji? Where are the banners demanding 'Majority Rule in the South Pacific'? The General Election campaign in Britain has shown once again how limitless are our national reserves of moral indignation.

I had returned to England to file an application for a UN Travel Document, and I did so in May. In fact, like all refugees, I had to purchase the Travel Document for £18. If the Adjudicator's comments made a good script for a Monty Python film, what followed now could be described only as a comedy of errors on the part of the authorities. On 13 June, I was unexpectedly served with notice to appear for a hearing before an adjudicator on 22 July 1994, with a strict warning that:

> If you do not appear at this hearing and fail to produce satisfactory explanation for your absence the adjudicator is empowered to proceed to hear the appeal on the evidence before him.

I immediately wrote a letter to the Adjudicator's Office but the office failed to respond to my written inquiry pertaining to the proposed appeal and administrative blunder. It did, however, notify Asylum Aid to ignore the Notice of Appeal No TH/4183/1994– Lal, R.V. (Appellant) and the Secretary of State (Respondent).

In June, two major personal events dominated my life. On 25 June I got married to my long-time Norwegian fiancée and the next day was I informed that my 22-year-old sister had died in Fiji in 'mysterious circumstances'. The latter tragic news devasted me. The tragedy was compounded with the fact that I could not attend her funeral services in Fiji – one of the most painful experiences of my exile. I had not seen her for over a decade and now never will again.

While I was still reeling from the shock of this unexpected bereavement, and the inability to console my widowed mother, I finally received my UN Travel Document. A close inspection of it however revealed that it contained an error regarding my occupational status. On the application form for a travel document, I had stated my occupation/profession as 'Writer and Academic' but the newly issued Travel Document listed my occupation as 'None'. Of course, I could have ignored the error but from what I had learnt from other refugees, I felt it ought to be corrected.

The refugees had related to me their harrowing experiences at the hands of immigration officials at European airports, and the great difficulty in convincing the officials that you have or have had a profession or occupation. The fact that my Travel Document suggested that I had no occupation or profession would immediately mark me out as a potential 'economic pest' in search of 'wealth' on the Continent. I strongly felt that since it was the Home Office which made the mistake in the first place, the Home Office must therefore make the requested correction.

I had earlier experienced at the hands of the German and Norwegian authorities the treatment the refugees had shared with me. At the German port city of Kiel, I was held up for several hours because the port authorities were not convinced that I had gone all the way from Norway for a night's stay in their city. Worse still, after they could not find on their world map a country called Fiji, they accused me of forging my Fijian passport. They refused to believe that the ticket that I had on me was won in a TV competition which had promised 'an exciting night in Kiel'.

The trip was indeed 'exciting' and the inhumane treatment beyond comparison. The German authorities, at last, threw the passport into my face, even though I had a three-day visa from the German embassy in Norway. I said to myself: 'Welcome to Kiel – Nazi German style'. I was the only one to suffer this indignity, for I was the only coloured man on the cruise liner.

In Norway, the customs officials had earlier abused me for using a baggage trolley set aside for journalists (I had not seen the label on the trolley, and in any case, the occupation on my Fiji passport stated 'Journalist'). It did not occur to them that a coloured man could also be a journalist. Also, I overheard two immigration officials muttering: 'Can't this Sri Lankan be in his own country'. I had arrived in Norway from England – and not Sri Lanka – to take up the prestigious Guest Nobel Fellowship at the Norwegian Nobel Institute in Oslo.

In late June 1994, I once again enlisted the help of the former Tory minister, who immediately wrote to the Home Office about my occupational status. He also enquired if the Travel Document (with correction) could be returned as soon as possible as I urgently needed to travel to the United States for my sister's memorial service, especially organised for me since I could not attend her funeral in Fiji. The ex-minister wrote to the Home Office on 30 June. On 19 July, I personally visited the Travel Document Section at Lunar House in Croydon seeking amendment of occupational status. The visit, the maltreatment, the atmosphere, and the perspiration/frustration in the crowded Lunar House could only be described as 'A Day at the Lunatic House'.

I left Oxford at about 5 am, only to find myself right at the back of the queue, for many had been camping outside since 3 am in the morning. When I was finally called to the counter at 4.30 pm, I was really disappointed to learn from the official – an African – that 'unofficial' Home Office policy was to state the occupation of Travel Document holders as 'none'.

I also learnt that, although I was now a married man and that the marital status and maiden and forenames of wife are requested on the Travel Document, the Home Office policy was not to enter these details. (These days I have a lot of explaining to do about my marital status to the Norwegian authorities, especially during the random police stop and search of illegal foreigners – 'aliens from outside Norway'– unless of course I carry on me the original marriage certificate).

The African official at Lunar House also claimed that in any case he could not attend to my enquiries because my file was with the Immigration Appeals Tribunal. I tried to explain the administrative mix-up and blunder on the part of the Adjudicator's Office and the urgent need to travel to the United States but he refused to listen to me. I then tried to explain to another official – an Asian – but she also refused to listen to me. The two refused to convey my enquiries to their white superiors sitting just behind the counter. The African official instead retained the recently issued Travel Document and advised me to phone the Home Office Enquiry Line. The retention of the Travel Document was acknowledged with an explanatory note that 'the above matter is receiving attention and the document will be returned as soon as possible – please keep inquiries about your case to a minimum'.

At the end of the bus journey back to Oxford, I concluded that I had wasted the whole day at the Home Office. I had only decided to call at Lunar House because I just could not get hold of anyone on the telephone (0181 760-2345). Over the years I had developed immunity to Home Office blunders and so presumably had others in similar circumstances. But on 19 July I heard at least one angry, frustrated, perspiring asylum seeker, who had just been forced out by the security guards, scream: 'This place is not Lunar House. It's bloody Lunatic House'. I, for once, understood him. The pain and humiliation was exacerbated by the fact that our own people – the Asians and Africans – whom the angry asylum-seeker branded as 'white minions' or 'gate-keepers' on behalf of the British government, had taken it upon themselves on 19 July to determine the justification of my complaint and enquiries.

On 22 July I finally managed to get through to the Travel Document Section. I was informed that the file was still in another department. It would take six to eight weeks to attend to the complaint and the proposed change regarding occupational status. I had already cancelled my planned honeymoon and now it seemed as if I had to call off the memorial service in memory of my sister (which I did).

On 25 July I decided to write directly to Michael Howard, the Home Secretary, whose post involved overseeing the implementation of immigration laws that included the controversial new Asylum and Immigration Bill. In the letter I explained the background of my case, the mistake on the Travel Document, the need to visit the US, my research travel plans, and above all, to visit my wife who was now pregnant and staying with her parents in Norway. But I was really disappointed to read the next day's headline in *The Times* (26 July), 'Major rewards Cabinet with extended holiday'. While I remained stranded in England with a UN Travel Document after seven long gruelling years, the newspapers were reporting that 'John Major has given his reshaped ministerial team permission to take longer summer holidays after a gruelling political year'.

The Times disclosed: 'France is again a popular destination for senior politicians. *Michael Howard, the Home Secretary, has led the way, setting off at the weekend.*' (my italics). I never heard from his office.

In late August I finally received the amended Travel Document. On 20 September, I received a copy of a letter sent to the former Tory Minister by the new Home Office Minister. In it, he notified the ex-Minister that the Travel Document was now in my possession, and that I withdrew my appeal against the original decision when I was granted full refugee status. He went on to note that, 'the appeal was withdrawn on 21 March but, unfortunately, the necessary paperwork was not completed until after a hearing date had been set. The adjudicator has, however, accepted that the appeal has been withdrawn'. The letter concluded with a familiar apology, 'I am very sorry for any confusion this oversight has caused to Mr Lal'.

He did not bother to comment or elaborate on the catalogue of errors on the part of the Home Office over a seven year period.

Thus ended a gruelling saga of the ordeal (and the peril) of applying for political asylum in England. I was initially given permission to stay in the United Kingdom for four years, after which I may apply for permanent settlement. Ironically, my application for political asylum had been considered during the most virulent debate on the law of asylum and refugees in Europe. In England, legislation after legislation was tabled against the so-called flood of refugees. The rapidly growing backlog of unresolved cases had led to an announcement by the British government in July 1991 that it would be introducing measures to speed up the asylum determination process, and to reduce the scope for misuse of the system. A Bill was introduced in the autumn of that year, but had not completed its passage through Parliament when the General Election of April was called. The Government reintroduced the Bill in November 1992 and it was passed the next year. At the time of writing, Michael Howard pushed through a slightly modified new Bill on immigration and asylum which, as one newspaper columnist, Miles Kingston, wrote in *The Independent* on 15 December 1995, 'would have excluded Michael Howard's Romanian parents from coming to Britain'.

But there are others who bitterly and shamelessly feel that the Bill is not radical enough because no one has a right to asylum in Great Britain. Bruce Anderson (*The Times*, 8 December 1995) argued:

> Political asylum is a 19th century idea, predating modern communications, air travel and welfare benefits. It assumed that a few heroic individuals who had wrestled unsuccessfully with tyranny would reach these shores, and that posterity would vindicate the decision to admit them ... At a guess, at least 100 million people would now meet the Geneva Convention criteria for asylum, having a well-grounded fear of persecution by reason of race, religion or nationality. ... But there is nothing we can do to help them. We are not prepared to wreck our own way of life to relieve their sufferings, and it is sentimental nonsense to pretend otherwise. By subscribing to the Geneva Convention, we are agreeing to a commitment which we have neither the intention nor the means to honour. So let us clear both our minds and our international obligations of cant, and find a new basis for asylum policy.

A series of legal judgements concerning refugees, and issues affecting them, are also extremely disturbing and, in the context of my own experiences, contrary to the claims and justifications of the British courts. On 19 January 1996, for example, Justice Latham rejected the application against deportation of the student son of a pro-democracy activist sent back to Nigeria and unheard of since. In ruling against the application of 20 year old Ade Onibiyo, Justice Latham rejected Onibiyo's plea that the Home Secretary, Michael Howard, had 'unreasonably and unlawfully' refused to consider his fresh claim for asylum or to allow him an appeal to a special adjudicator. Judge Latham ruled that the Home Secretary had been entitled to conclude in December that Onibiyo's renewed application 'did not constitute a fresh claim' and did not disclose any material which justified the Home Secretary reversing his earlier decision. The judge went further and, in a decision with important general implications for asylum seekers, ruled that those allegedly fleeing persecution were entitled to have only one claim considered by the United Kingdom immigration authorities before having to leave this country. Onibiyo was, however, given leave to appeal because, according to the judge, 'It seems to me to be a time it was grappled with in the Court of Appeal' (*The Independent*, 20 January 1996). On 28 March the Court of Appeal upheld Howard's decision. The three judges ruled that it was for the Home Secretary, not the courts, to rule whether an applicant could demonstrate 'a relevant and substantial change in circumstances' justifying a fresh claim. Howard had properly exercised his powers in concluding that there was no 'fresh claim'.

If one considers my seven year battle for asylum, especially after the first rejection of my application, it is frightening to contemplate what would have been my fate in Fiji under the new ruling that an asylum seeker is entitled to have only one claim considered by the UK immigration authorities before having to leave Great Britain.

In February, the British government also successfully fought off legal attempts to halt its scheme to withdraw benefits from those who are appealing against an initial refusal for asylum, which can take months (in my case seven years), and to those who do not apply for asylum the moment they arrive in the United Kingdom. The government claims it will save £200 million a year and is calculated to deter bogus applications. Mr Justice Brooke ruled that he had no powers to grant a stay or an injunction until the case could be heard. Earlier, the Joint Council for the Welfare of Immigrants (JCWI) had mounted the legal challenge, claiming that the decision of the Social Security Secretary, Peter Lilley, to withdraw benefits, income support and other benefits from asylum seekers was *ultra vires*. The application for judicial review claimed that Lilley had no power to use social security regulations to curtail asylum seekers' rights. It argued that those who were homeless and without means would be physically and mentally incapable of presenting evidence to support their claims or appeals. The judicial challenge argued the decision would breach Britain's international obligations under the United Nations Conventions on Refugees and on the Rights of the Child. Claude Moraes of the Joint Council for the Welfare of Immigrants said:

> These are the most brutal and shocking proposals we have seen in the 29 years of our history. We have a duty to continue the fight in the courts. This measure will mean we will see individual tragedies on a daily basis.

Social Security Secretary Lilley, on the other hand, claimed the regulations were necessary to ensure Britain remained a safe haven for those genuinely fleeing persecution, to speed up the processing of asylum claims, and to discourage unfounded claims from economic migrants (*The Guardian*, 5 February 1996). The rules, approved by Parliament, were introduced by Lilley as part of efforts to deter thousands of 'bogus claims by asylum seekers, who enter for economic reasons rather than to escape persecution'. The British government has argued that the onus is on refugees to establish that they have a genuine claim. They are not entitled to be treated as refugees, with the advantages that that entails, until they have done so, it claimed. At the heart of the legal challenge was the claim that the new regulations were contrary to domestic law and in breach of articles of the 1951 Geneva Convention. Initially, the JCWI had won a temporary permission for the new rules to be challenged in the High Court. Mr Justice Brooke had ruled that there was 'an arguable case' that asylum seekers were entitled to be treated as refugees, and consequently entitled to benefits, unless and until it was proved that their claims were bogus. He was not commenting on the merits of the British government's case (*The Daily Telegraph*, 7 February 1996).

On 24 June 1996, the Court of Appeal, however, ruled that the denial of welfare to would-be refugees was 'uncivilised' and 'inhumane' and outlawed the withdrawal of their welfare benefits. The court ruled that Peter Lilley had overstepped his powers by introducing regulatory rather than statutory changes in February. Lord Justice Simon Brown, in a two to one majority judgment, said that 'so basic were the human rights issues at stake' that they were illustrated in a 200 year old poor law ruling that a 'poor foreigner' was entitled to state 'relief to save them from starving'. According to Lord Justice Brown, 'Parliament cannot have intended a significant number of asylum-seekers to be impaled on the horns of so intolerable a dilemma: the need to either abandon their claims to refugee status or, alternatively, to maintain them as best they can but in a state of utter destitution'. He felt that 'no civilised nation can tolerate' the destitution of many would-be refugees.

Characteristically Roger Evans, the Social Security Minister, said the British Government would press ahead with the benefit changes, despite the ruling. They were necessary, he maintained, to stop bogus claims for refugee status from economic migrants who simply wanted to take advantage of Britain's welfare state as more than 90 per cent of asylum applications were currently found to be false (*The Independent*, 24 June 1996).

Furthermore, and in the context of my own case, the most far-reaching and potentially dangerous judgement was that of the House of Lords in the case of two Somali asylum seekers who claimed that the 'fast track' appeal machinery for challenging decisions by the Home Secretary was unfair. The five law lords decided on 15 February by a 3-2 majority that the Home Secretary, Michael Howard, was not obliged to disclose his grounds for ruling that their asylum applications were 'without foundation'. The two Somali's fast-track appeals to Special Adjudicators under the 1993 Asylum and Immigration Appeals Act were also rejected on grounds that there was no evidence to suggest that Spain was not a safe country to which they could be returned. The two had arrived in Britain in November 1993 after spending several days in Spain. Dismissing the appeals, Lord Lloyd of Berwick said he was not persuaded that justice required the Home Secretary to disclose the grounds for his decision. If the courts were to supplement the asylum appeals rules by imposing such an obligation, claimed Lord Lloyd, there would be a risk of frustrating the clear intention of Parliament that such appeals should be considered with all due speed. The two dissenting judges however argued that they would have upheld the appeals on the grounds that there was insufficient evidence for the special adjudicators to support the Home Secretary's ruling. Moreover, the Adjudicators needed all the relevant material available to carry out their duties and asylum seekers were required frankly to disclose relevant information to immigration officers and 'what is sauce for the goose is sauce for the gander'. Ironically, Lord Lloyd's assertion that asylum 'appeals should be considered with all due speed' appears to be a travesty of justice for, after all, justice is supposed to be blind! In other words, a sauce for a brutal murderer goose is also a sauce for a vulnerable asylum seeker gander.

    In summary, I would like to declare that it is not my intention to chastise the British government, the Home Office or the refugee and asylum policy in the United Kingdom. What I have attempted to do is to sketch in the human dimension of the ordeal (and the peril) in applying for political asylum in Great Britain. I have also declined to write the text in the usual academic genre. Personal suffering cannot be narrated/measured, or even conveyed, in terms of academic substance. The main purpose is to provide a cohesive account of a personal saga of what would otherwise remain concealed in Home Office files or otherwise be a fragmentary and uneven academic commentary in the field of refugee studies.

Moreover, I have used the word 'refugee' with some hesitation. Circumstances beyond my control had forced me to take refuge in Great Britain. It was the only route open to me, the only honourable way forward that would enable me to rebuild my shattered life and career in another country, to continue to fight for freedom and justice in my own country and also those who want to be free to choose their own destiny. The narrative is, above all, a record of personal suffering and moral strength, and a summons to others in a similar predicament not to give up hope.

Put in the most simple way, if the two racist coups in Fiji had changed the course of my life, so did England's pariah-like treatment of me. In 1984 I was accorded a near royal reception because I had come from the so-called paradise island to study. A decade later, in 1994, I was being treated like an outcast of the old Empire because now I was asking the British government to provide me political sanctuary from a racist dictator stalking that troubled paradise.

Overall, in my seven-year struggle for political asylum, from 1987 to 1994, I saw Britain change one Prime Minister (Margaret Thatcher) for another (John Major). My fate passed through the hands of four Home Secretaries': Douglas Hurd, Kenneth Baker, Kenneth Clarke and finally Michael Howard. The last is the son of a Romanian Jewish refugee, who acquired the name Howard to make assimilation into Welsh culture easier and, subsequently, entry into the corridors of political power in the United Kingdom. In any case, the modern definition of a refugee was formulated largely in response to European refugee flows, to accommodate the likes of Howard's refugee father. Although Article 14 of the Universal Declaration of Human Rights states that, 'Every one has the right to seek and enjoy in other countries asylum from persecution', the Declaration has no binding force. In other words, GREAT Britain is not compelled to implement it.

In August 1994 I returned to Norway on a UN Travel Document issued by the British government. As I landed in Norway, the birthplace of Nobel laureate Fridtjof Nansen (1861–1930), the man who had conceived the very idea of a travel document for refugees, I reflected at the end of a long journey from *reporter* to *refugee* the sentiments in the 'Song of Exile' (Paul Tabori, *The Anatomy of Exile: A Semantic and Historical Study*, G. Harrap, London, 1972):

> Exile is the eruption whose lava stream
> carries you away
> Exile is the warning example to those who
> still have their homes, who belong.
> But will you take heed of the warning?
> Exile is the escape that is often worse than the prison.

It must be also stated that the right to travel on a UN Travel Document does not provide you the right to protection, as the document states:

> The issue of this travel document does not entitle the holder to the protection of British diplomatic or consular representatives in foreign countries. Nor does it convey exemption from any of the regulations concerning foreign nationals living in, or travelling in and out of, the United Kingdom.

The Travel Document is however silent on the conduct of Immigration Officers empowered to deal with out-going and incoming *bona fide* refugees, as I found out on 19 May 1996 at Heathrow Airport in London.

I had returned to England after an absence of nearly two years, but this time I was accompanied by my wife and our fifteen month old baby daughter, Bianca. While my wife and baby, as Norwegian citizens, were let in without a single question, I was immediately subjected to the routine cross-examination regarding the nature and circumstances of my obtaining refugee status, questions which I thought were completely irrelevant and had been effectively settled in 1994. But what really surprised me was the highly inflammatory and unwarranted remarks of the Immigration Officer at Heathrow airport. He ventured to suggest as follows: 'I see, you can't go back to Fiji. I know why the indigenous Fijians don't like you Indians because you have taken over their country.' Burning with concealed anger, and my baby uncontrollably screaming for me in the EC zone, I retorted: 'No! You are completely wrong. We have not taken over the country. My problem with the Government of Fiji is political and moral. Anyway, your unwarranted comments have no relevance to my entry requirements.'. He seemed to have got the message but I asked myself: What is his personal view on the so-called naturalized and non-white immigrants in Great Britain? For the strength of the prejudice and perception of a people, it can be argued, is measured by its response to 'invasion by aliens' from a foreign land, a slogan, in fact, so effectively used by a group of racist Fijian political leaders to terrorize and brutalize the Indo-Fijian community in Fiji.

By way of conclusion, what really prevented me from suffering a complete physical and mental breakdown at the hands of the British Home Office? In one sentence, the belief in inner freedom, a freedom which allowed me a freedom to dream that there was at the end of the dark tunnel a strong light (i.e. an overwhelming evidence in my favour) which would enable me to escape from the 'bureaucratic prison' of the Home Office, and I certainly did 'escape': in the form of a bona fide UN Convention refugee. In the words of the former Russian Jewish human rights activist Nathan Sharansky (*The Times*, 6 February 1990):

> The most important thing is to hear the free soul within ourselves. But you see, people don't often let themselves hear their soul freely. It was this sense of inner freedom that I found in the prisons of the Soviet Union which kept me alive and which will keep me alive.

I am, however, still walking on the long highway to real freedom, and am still hoping to complete the last leg of the unfinished journey: to visit my birthplace in Fiji, the burial grounds of my late father and my beloved sister which I have never seen, and to be able to sing freely with my fellow Fiji citizens the pre-coup national anthem which hailed Fiji as a land of freedom and multi-racialism:

Blessing grant, oh God of Nations, on the isles of Fiji,
As we stand united under noble banner blue,
Shores of golden sand and sunshine, happiness and song,
And we honour and defend the cause of freedom ever

Stand united, we of Fiji, fame and glory ever,
Onward march together, God bless Fiji.

For Fiji, ever Fiji, let our voices ring with pride,
For Fiji, ever Fiji, her name hail far and wide,
A land of freedom, hope and glory, to endure whatever befall,
May God bless Fiji for evermore.

In parting, perhaps the most salutary message of what is an otherwise intensely personal asylum saga, is the poignant reminder that *Exile* is a song that only the singer can hear, but *Cry Freedom* is a universal song that the world can and must share. As Nelson Mandela put it in his autobiography *Long Walk to Freedom*: 'I was not born with a hunger to be free – I was born free.'

Victor Lal
June 1996, Norway